A YEAR IN THE LIFE OF A CIVIL WAR SOLDIER

A NOVEL
BASED ON THE DIARY OF
SILAS NEWTON CROSS

by Diana Loski
illustrations by Linda Sniffen and Jolie Kemp

published by

WRITERS PRESS
Boise, Idaho 83714

For
John R. Halderman,
my father, friend, and fellow Civil War buff,

and for
Silas Newton Cross,
in loving memory.

AUTHOR'S NOTE

The story you are about to read actually occurred. Fiction has been used in parts to tie together incomplete details, and the characterizations are of my own making. But the people were real, the battles and events that led to them actually happened, and the tragic war that took place between 1861 and 1865 left scars that are still felt today.

By the year 1864, which was considered by many Americans who lived then as the darkest of years, Silas Newton Cross had served in the Union infantry for two years. His regiment took part in the Red River Siege in Louisiana under the command of General Nathaniel Banks. When that failed, Silas boarded a steamer for Virginia and served under Philip Sheridan and Ord's Army of the James in the Shenandoah Valley.

Many generals are mentioned in the book, and none of them are fictitious. Many of the various generals' quotes in the book were their actual words, according to Silas's diary. It is my hope that all the commanding officers aren't confusing. The army was broken down into corps, divisions, brigades, and regiments. All but regiments were commanded by generals. Colonels led regiments and, sometimes, brigades. Regiments were broken down further into companies headed by captains. Sometimes as many as fifteen companies made up a regiment, but by 1864 the number of men had dwindled, and some companies ceased to exist.

Whenever possible, I used Silas's own terms, such as "dog tent" and "stone pike." I also provided some of the slang terms which were used in the diary and common in the 1800's. The expression "men of color" isn't an attempt at political correctness. It was used in the nineteenth century to describe Black Americans. The Corps d'Afrique, made up of men of color, fought alongside the Union troops in the battle of Sabine Crossroads near Mansfield, Louisiana, the cumulative battle of the Red River Siege.

I would like to thank Gwynne Wolverton, owner of the diary and Silas's descendant, for bringing the diary to my publisher. She spent many weeks transcribing the diary, decoding nineteenth century spelling and lettering, and thus rendering the task of writing Silas's story much easier for me.

I appreciate the following authors and their books for helping me bring Silas's story to life: Shelby Foote's *Civil War, Vol. 3, Red River to Appomatox*, the Pulitzer Prize winning *The Killer Angels* by Michael Shaara, *The Passing of the Armies* by Joshua L. Chamberlain, and *Civil War Times* magazine.

Most of all, I am grateful to Silas and the thousands of soldiers like him, Union and Confederate, who took a little time each day to write about their places in history. Hopefully their words will continue to speak to us, ensuring that an event like the one in 1864 will never occur again.

This book is dedicated to the memory of Silas Newton Cross, a valiant Civil War soldier. I didn't realize what an adventure transcribing his diary would bring. As I worked, I was able to visualize where he went and what transpired in his world in 1864. I discovered what kind of man my great-great grandfather was, a young man fighting for his beliefs in a torn land.

He made friends of strangers he met along the way. He enjoyed life by reading, writing, fishing, and sightseeing when the war gave him the precious time to do so.

I am filled with pride and wonder for a man I never had the opportunity to know.

Thanks to my children: Sandy, Debbie, and Mike for their assistance; and to Kelly Behrens for his patience and encouragement.

Gwynne Wolverton

"We are liberty covered with dust."

Silas Newton Cross
October 8, 1864

CHAPTER ONE

January 22, 1864

Corporal Silas Cross sat on the shore of Lake Pontchartrain, awestruck. The sunrise spilled gold on the purple waters so beautifully it took his breath away. He ran his hand through his thick black hair, his serious brown eyes drinking in the dawn. Iowa was nothing like this place.

A gangly blue heron, which reminded Silas of Ol' Abe, fished in the shallows. Silas smiled.

"Up a little early this morning," he said softly, more to himself than to the bird.

He felt hungry. Salt pork and corn bread sounded good right now, even if they did eat the same thing day after day. Most of the troops complained, especially about the corn bread, but Silas always kept to himself, eating quietly. Corn bread beat hardtack as far as he was concerned. Perhaps today he would hunt again for his regiment. Last week he snagged a white-tail deer, common in the Louisiana bayous. Maybe today, like the heron, he would go fishing. Unless they were moving on.

"I thought I would find you here, friend."

Silas turned his head slowly and looked calmly at the stubby, sharp-featured man with light brown hair and piercing blue eyes. No one ever startled Silas Newton Cross. All the 28th Iowa liked him. His cool head had kept him, and many around him, alive for over two years.

"Hi, Henry," Silas replied. "What brings you here at this hour? It's a good twenty minutes before reveille."

"I spotted sutler's wagons just over the hill. Thought you might want to know. You never can tell what they might be bringin'."

Silas continued staring at the lake. The sun rose slowly from the horizon, casting the gentle light of day on everything it touched. It was probably snowing at home.

"I suppose every huckster from miles around will be with the wagon," Silas said.

"Ah, well, who can blame them?" Henry asked, stroking the reddish stubble on his chin. "They're just tryin' to earn their livelihood."

Silas nodded. War brought people together under the strangest of circumstances. Like his friendship with Henry. They were years apart in age. Silas was nineteen and Henry was over thirty—and they were a lifetime apart in everything else. Whereas Silas had been raised with traditions, values, and devotion to family, Henry had grown up alone, fighting for food and shelter nearly every day of his life with no one to turn to. Ever. Silas had joined the 28th Iowa because it was his duty, and because he thought he was embarking on a great adventure. Henry, on the other hand, saw it as survival. A monthly wage and regular meals. Silas almost laughed out loud. Seeing war as survival. How ridiculous. And yet it was true.

"Let's get back," Henry said, interrupting his thoughts. "That horn'll be blaring any minute. I hear we're moving on today."

"The Sarge has said that for three days now," Silas replied. "I'll believe it when I see the boats myself."

"Well, you probably will be the one to spot 'em," Henry declared, "seein' you're always out here at dawn, staring at this dad-blamed lake."

"I like to watch the sunrise."

"Take it from me, Silas, you see one sunrise, you've seen 'em all." Henry turned abruptly and headed for camp.

Silas stood slowly, brushing dried grass from his trousers. He was already dressed in full uniform: a dark blue jacket fastened with brass buttons, with two chevrons on each sleeve. His powder blue trousers wore a narrow, yellow stripe down the sides. Black brogans covered his feet. He bent over and reached for his Enfield rifle. He never went anywhere without it. The days had been mostly dull and eventless since Vicksburg, but the Rebels sometimes showed up without warning. Silas had learned never to be caught off guard.

He strode into camp just as the trumpet called. The sleeping camp sprang to life. Men, most of them bleary-eyed, crawled out of dog tents and blankets. Silas knew it was because they stayed up late into the night playing cards. Silas didn't waste his time with gaming. He knew the other soldiers were far better at it than he, and he wasn't eager to part with his hard-earned income. He usually read by candlelight or wrote letters or served on picket duty.

He saw the sutler setting up his cart in an open field. His stomach rumbled in response to the strong, salty smell of bacon traveling on the breeze from the makeshift kitchen in camp. Anthony, their cook, was pretty good at creating decent meals. Silas hoped he would stay but didn't think Anthony would do so. The cooks, usually men of color like Anthony, didn't remain long in camp. They either fled north to ensure freedom in otherwise uncertain circumstances or joined the Corps d'Afrique. So far, Anthony had stayed the longest—about six weeks.

Silas walked to the sutler's wagon. A dozen people, mostly Creole women and children clad in rags, swarmed around it, blocking his view of the merchandise.

"Buy some nice jewelry, Mister? I sell it cheap."

"Tobacco for sale. A dollar a plug."

Silas passed by them without a word. He tried to avoid their gaze, especially the children. Their huge black eyes bored into his, evoking a deep, silent groan from within him. In the beginning he had given to them, but more and more came after, always thinner and hungrier than the others. He finally realized it was hopeless. He strode up to the sutler, a small, thin man with white hair and yellow teeth.

"How much for eggs?" Silas asked. Scrambled eggs for breakfast, along with bacon, sounded delectable. He hadn't eaten eggs since he enlisted.

"Thirty-five cents apiece," the sutler replied.

Silas didn't flinch. "That's highway robbery," he said quietly.

"The price is just gonna go up," the sutler answered matter-of-factly. "If I was you, I'd buy now."

Sure, Silas thought. Sutlers always said that. But sometimes their lies proved true. The past year had been full of alternate periods of famine and plenty. He pulled out a quarter and a dime.

"I'll take one," he said. He almost took a pound of butter, too, but thought better of it. If Henry were right about moving out, it would just be a waste of money.

Silas wove through the increasing crowd, carefully shielding his cherished egg in his hands. He saw the rest of his regiment lining up outside the mess tent. The sun cast a golden glow on the camp, giving it an almost homey, appealing air. Brass buttons on blue jackets and bayonets glinted in the early light. He stepped into line, still holding his egg.

He reached Anthony at last. The cook, dressed in a worn, oversized shirt and trousers covered with a soiled apron, grinned. His perfect teeth were strikingly white against his ebony skin.

"Hey, Silas," Anthony said.

"Hello, Anthony," Silas replied. He held up his egg. "Can you cook this real quick for me?"

Silas could tell Anthony was impressed.

"You decided to splurge, I see," the cook said with a sly smile.

Silas turned up the corners of his mouth only slightly.

"How you want it?"

"Scrambled," Silas said.

Anthony whipped up Silas's breakfast in moments: bacon and egg, hot corn bread, and black coffee. Silas walked to a secluded spot outside, in view of the lake, and ate voraciously.

When he was finished he leaned back, placing his tin cup and plate on the grass. The sun was a burning yellow ball over the lake now. He looked at the calm blue waters and noticed a speck in the distance. He stood on his feet, shielding his eyes from the sun with the back of his hand for a better look.

It was definitely a boat—but for which side? Confederate gun boats patrolled the rivers and lakes, blasting Union keel boats and camps with artillery. Most likely, though, it was the schooner to ferry them across Lake Pontchartrain to Madisonville.

Silas crouched behind the abundant shrubbery and watched. As the ship drew closer, Silas breathed a small sigh of relief.

They were going to Madisonville.

CHAPTER TWO

January 24, 1864

Madisonville was a quiet resort town of about three hundred inhabitants before twelve hundred soldiers marched in. Once a playground for the elite of New Orleans, it was rapidly becoming a makeshift fortress for the Union Army.

Silas split wood and dug ditches in the cool sunshine until his shoulders ached. He stopped to rest in the shade. The wonderful fragrance of freshly dug earth permeated the air. General Grover had ordered the fortifications up immediately, so Silas knew he couldn't rest long.

"Corporal."

Silas glanced up to see a man with chestnut hair and whiskers, looking lean and commanding in his frock coat. Lieutenant Dran's official demeanor and sharp blue eyes brought Silas to attention. "Applegate will relieve you. Return to camp to report for picket duty."

"Yes, sir." Silas saluted and left his shovel in the rich brown soil. He picked up his rifle and hurried back to camp. The immense waters of the lake glimmered in the late afternoon sun. The air filled with sounds of conversation and soft laughter, axes, and spades opening the earth.

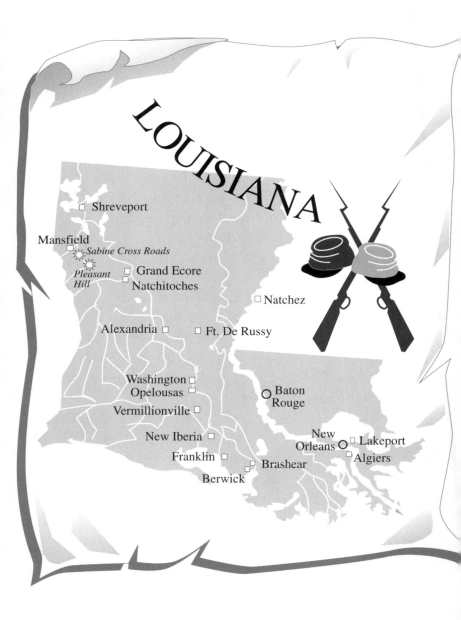

LOUISIANA

□ Shreveport

Mansfield
□ *Sabine Cross Roads*

Pleasant Hill   □ Grand Ecore
           □ Natchitoches

                          □ Natchez

Alexandria □   □ Ft. De Russy

      Washington □
      Opelousas □
                              ○ Baton
                                Rouge
   Vermillionville □

      New Iberia □   New   □ Lakeport
                            Orleans ○
      Franklin □   □ Algiers
              □ Brashear
      Berwick

LOUISIANA

Madisonville

New
Orleans ○ □ Lakeport

Algiers □

The map on the left page shows an overview of Louisiana. The inset above shows southern Louisiana, where Silas Cross and the rest of the 28th Iowa regiment were deployed following their duty in Vicksburg, Mississippi. After arriving in Madisonville, on the shores of Lake Pontchartrain, they became involved in the Red River Siege, a little-known but pivotal conflict of the Civil War.

9

As he entered camp, Silas caught sight of new recruits gathered in a huddle near the Colonel's tent, which was unmistakable among the small dog tents. A man could walk into Colonel Slack's tent without bending over. Silas smiled at the men, noticing their obviously forced nonchalance. The first sight of the huge camp was always overwhelming to new recruits. His smile turned into a grin when he recognized a familiar face.

"Keck!"

The young man, blond and sturdy looking, turned to Silas with widened eyes. It was Keckley, all right.

Silas felt a flood of relief and joy at seeing Keck again. He thought perhaps his friend had not recovered.

"Silas!" Keckley exclaimed. "I hoped you'd be here. With the war and all, well," he paused, "I wasn't sure."

"I'm still around as you can see. We'll all be here a while. There's a sawmill yonder that Grover thinks the Rebs will be needing for lumber." He eyed his friend. "You're looking well, Keck. How long has it been now?"

"I was home sixty days."

"And you're feeling all right? You seemed at Death's door when they shipped you out."

"I was pretty sick," Keckley agreed. "The typhoid darn near took me out. But, I'm fine now. I couldn't wait to get back."

Silas thought Keckley looked robust enough. Typhoid, dysentery, malaria, and smallpox claimed more lives than all the battles put together.

"Want to bunk with me again?" Silas asked. "I've had the tent all to myself since you left."

"Sure," Keckley said.

Silas picked up a black canvas knapsack. "Is this yours?"

Keckley nodded. "Yeah. And one of those blankets is mine, too," he said, gesturing to a gray wool blanket rolled up by several others of the same hue. Keck picked it up and followed Silas to the small white dog tent surrounded by hundreds of others just like it.

They entered the tent on their knees, crouching to keep from bumping their heads on its roof, in the usual silence typical of Silas Cross. Finally Keckley spoke again.

"I hear we're heading up to Shreveport."

Silas nodded. "Banks has ordered a siege on the graybacks' stronghold there," he said. "Vicksburg handled a good deal of their supplies to the armies, but not all. I hear Texas sends wheat, beans, coffee, and cotton for uniforms and such to Shreveport. From there it goes out on the gulf to wherever Bobby Lee and Jeff Davis want it to go."

Keckley whistled softly. "Sounds like we're gonna see some action."

"We sure will." Silas grabbed his rifle. "I got picket duty, Keck. What are you going to do?"

"I have to report to Colonel Slack."

"See you then," Silas said.

"See ya."

Silas walked to the tangled vegetation of swamp land on the west side of camp. He saw Henry sitting on the large rock which marked their post, whittling a piece of wood slowly and carefully.

"I'm here to relieve you, Henry," Silas said.

Henry slid off the rock. "It's been pretty quiet."

Silas smiled. "Hope it stays that way."

Henry shrugged. "They usually attack us at dawn or dusk. So, watch it when the sun sets, Silas. Don't be starin' at that lake and get caught unawares." He emitted a short, listless laugh.

Silas said nothing and leaned his back against the cold gray stone. The men in camp called it "Stonewall." They were just too funny, Silas thought.

CHAPTER THREE

February 11, 1864

Silas sat in his tent reading a Waverly magazine Keckley had brought from home. He never read them much before. They had been a waste of time at home with all the chores to finish. Now he seemed to have too much time.

His mind wandered to his home in Clinton. He saw the white farm house that his grandfather Cross had built with his own hands and the whitewashed fence surrounding it. The barn and silo were white, too, blending subtly with the wheat and providing a sharp contrast to green stalks of corn. He remembered the cold mornings when he rose at four to milk the cows and slop the hogs. The city boys couldn't understand why Silas was up daily before reveille. But Silas's day always began before dawn, and it always would.

A gaunt private, scarcely more than fifteen, entered the tent.

"A mail for you, Corporal."

Silas took the letter, his calm demeanor masking the relief he felt. He had not heard from home in over three weeks. Father wrote most often. Silas loved his father, distantly. The miles separating them in war brought them closer than when they had been on the farm. Albert Cross was quiet and hardworking, and like his son, a man of few words. Silas's mother, Elizabeth, was much more given to displays of affection.

Silas recognized the handwriting on the envelope. John, his fifteen-year-old brother, had written this time. Silas tore open the flap and pulled out the letter.

Jan. 29, 1864

Dear Silas,

We hope you are well. I have been begging Father to let me enlist so I can be with you. But he says I'm needed more at the farm. The winter wheat is growing tall. We should harvest it late next month. Old Rosie is going to calf sometime in the spring.

Ma had a hard time without you at Christmas. She knitted you a stocking cap. Did you ever get it? Father says you're down in bayou country where it's warm and won't need it anyway.

If you could write us and tell Father how much you need soldiers, maybe he'll let me enlist. Give it a try will you?

Your brother,
John

Silas folded the letter neatly and placed it in his haversack. He shook his head. Louisiana wasn't always warm, though some days had been like spring. He never received the stocking cap. He wondered if he should tell his mother he got it anyway, but decided against it.

He heard a series of pops followed by the all-too-familiar shriek of the Rebel yell. He jumped up and grabbed his rifle. Men were running amok through camp, the officers in command shouting for order. Silas quickly fell in line with the rapidly forming group and marched with them in the direction of the gunfire.

He felt strangely calm. He always did in skirmishes. The Confederates almost always attacked this way— surprise attacks from the thick growth of trees and brackish swamps—a far cry from the famous battles others fought in Virginia, Gettysburg, and Tennessee. They were smart, Silas admitted to himself. Silas's regiment probably outnumbered them three to one, but the Rebs knew the country—which greatly increased their odds against the Union army.

Silas caught a fragmented glimpse of gray behind the trees. Puffs of smoke emanated from the tangled forests of bald cypress crowned with Spanish moss. He saw a few men ahead of him drop to the ground, motionless. Within moments he was among the trees, soldiers in blue beside him, his heart beating in his throat.

The whistle of minie balls drowned out the distant shouts and groans of his comrades. He crouched low, weaving his way into the forest. Men in gray, as well as some in brown-dyed uniforms called butternuts, popped up out of nowhere; then disappeared just as quickly. Silas noticed that some were barefoot, their clothes tattered like the waifs he'd seen at the sutler's cart. He dropped to one knee by a large cottonwood, the moss hanging from its branches like shredded cobwebs, and waited.

He didn't have to wait long. A young Confederate, his brown hair curled around his innocent face, peeked out from behind the thick brush, aiming dead-on at Silas's chest.

Silas shot first. He heard a cry of pain. The boy clutched his shoulder and, dropping his gun, ran for cover. Silas crouched behind the tree. His aim had been perfect. The boy was too young. Maybe now he would go home and work on his farm somewhere in Louisiana, or perhaps Mississippi, where he belonged. Just like John. Silas knew his brother was where he belonged, too.

The forest grew suddenly quiet. The Rebs had disappeared to fight them in the same fashion on another day.

Silas remained behind the tree and reloaded. He reached into his cartridge box for the cartridge containing the gunpowder and minie ball. He ripped the paper with his teeth and poured the silty powder into the barrel. He pushed the bullet into the barrel with his thumb. He pulled the ramrod out of its place on the barrel and used it to push down the ammunition.

He heard a rustling noise. He froze.

A man, his gray uniform matching the steely hardness of his eyes, stood fearlessly before Silas. He held his rifle, and had an extra rifle slung over his shoulder.

The man raised his rifle to Silas's chest as Silas scrambled to pull back the hammer on his Enfield.

Silas felt his heart stop as he heard the pop of gunfire. The soldier before him fell soundlessly to the ground.

Another man in blue stepped out of the clumps of green.

Silas looked up into Henry's stubbly face. His heart sprang to life again, hammering furiously.

"Thanks, Henry," he whispered. "I owe you."

Henry grabbed the two rifles, one still clutched in the dead man's hands.

"We can use these," he said. "Besides, we don't want the Rebs to have 'em." He stood, flinging the rifles onto his back.

"Well, come on," Henry said.

Silas stood slowly, his eyes fixed on the ghastly heap before him. He had come too close today. All because he took pity on a boy. Henry would call him a fool if he knew.

"I'm coming," Silas replied.

Chapter Four

February 18, 1864

    Silas and Keckley woke to a thin blanket of white over their camp. Silas opened the flap and felt the cold air sting his cheeks. If only he had the stocking cap now. They had been confined to camp for three days as the torrential rains beat upon the boys in blue. Many soldiers were sick because of the adverse weather and the poor rations. The last few days they were reduced to eating crackers or hardtack three times a day. Silas's stomach rumbled as he listened to the trumpet call. At least there would be hot coffee in the morning.

    He and Keckley dressed in silence and strode out into the winter landscape

    They no longer drilled in the morning before break-fast. Sergeant Jones had explained they all needed their strength for the march toward Shreveport, which would continue as soon as the weather cleared. There was talk of joining General McClernand in Texas. The mill would be abandoned. Silas's face remained stonelike when he heard the news. No one would stay behind to ensure the Rebs couldn't use it. No one moved together or saw anything through. General Banks was an idiot. He was sure the Confederate and Union soldiers were in agreement on that fact.

The strong smell of grease made his stomach turn as he and Keckley entered the mess tent. Anthony was gone, and in his place a thickly built Creole cooked slapjacks over a stove.

Silas grimaced as the greasy fried cakes fell heavily onto his plate. He filled his tin cup with hot coffee, inhaling deeply the strong, pleasant smell to offset the acrid odor of grease rising from his plate. He walked over to Henry and Joe Skeels, a pudgy private from Des Moines, who sat outside the tent by one of the many campfires to stay warm.

"Morning," Silas said as he joined his mess group.

Henry and Joe, busily stuffing their mouths full of slapjacks, nodded congenially.

Silas drank from his cup as Keckley joined them.

"This cooking ain't like Ma's, is it, boys?" Keck joked.

"Does anyone know where Anthony went?" Silas asked.

Henry swallowed a mouthful and immediately stuffed another piece of slapjack between his teeth. "Dunno," he said. "Probably went up north. Who cares?"

Silas felt slightly wounded by the words but made sure his face didn't betray him. He probably shouldn't care, but he did. "Anthony was the best cook we've had in a long time," he said simply. He looked at the lumps of flour and salt swimming in grease and took a long drink of his coffee.

Keck took a bite of his breakfast. "If the ague doesn't get us, this stuff sure will," he said with a laugh.

By noon the snow had melted. Silas read an old Waverly magazine Joe loaned him while Keckley wrote home.

"I'm askin' Ma to send some recipes," Keckley said.

Silas scoffed. "Why? So you can give them to that cook?" He had only taken one bite of his breakfast and decided that was enough. Rations would be coming soon. Or, he would go hunting again.

Keckley laughed. "No. But I can cook a little. I used to help Ma can fruit and pickle cucumbers in the fall. Cooking is easy. You just follow the recipe."

Silas turned back to his magazine. No one thought of recipes at a time like this! No one but Keckley.

The rest of the day passed lazily. By the time he reported for picket duty, Silas had written three letters; read a dime novel, also loaned by Joe, entitled *Seth Jones*; and played two games of draw poker with Keckley. Silas won both games with two pair and a full house. Keckley was easy to beat. Silas wrote in his diary as dusk fell, then picked up his rifle for sentry duty.

An endless black sky studded with stars greeted him as he took his place by the large gray stone. The night air chilled him. He rubbed his arms vigorously under his uniform to keep warm. In the distance he saw the glow of campfires and heard a comforting mix of fiddle music, singing, and laughter. The boys were ready to enjoy some merriment after their long confinement.

He leaned back against the stone, its coldness like a ball of ice in his back. He shifted his rifle to cushion his back from "ol' Stonewall," then returned to the same position, his eyes fixed on the distant fires, and sang quietly along with the music.

CHAPTER FIVE

March 1, 1864

Silas sat on the ground beside Henry, Keckley, and Joe. He saw others of his regiment nearby—Sam Martin, Lawrence Applegate, Marcellus Conner, and a new recruit named McCane. The Nineteenth Corps, all twelve thousand of them, listened intently to General McClernand's speech.

Algiers, where they now camped, was a pleasant town on the Mississippi, just across the river from New Orleans. Silas could see the brick edifices of the city, with black, wrought-iron gates and white porticos, in the distance, through the scattered oaks and cypress. The Mississippi, a giant of a river, glistened lazily in the sun.

McClernand, a veteran of Shiloh and Vicksburg, looked imposing in his impeccable uniform. His black beard hid most of his sharp face. Thick black eyebrows shaded his piercing eyes. The sun's rays reflected on his forehead, making the receding hairline obvious to all, although a wealth of black hair hung to his neck in back.

"We're proud of you boys," he shouted so everyone could hear. "Your acts of bravery in the face of the enemy have reached us in Texas. I hope you will imitate these acts in the future. We'll sweep the west side clear of Rebs!!"

21

A deafening cheer rose from the crowd of soldiers.

A breath of wind bent the tall grasses as McClernand dismissed the troops and stepped down. A surge of soldiers overtook him like a wave upon sand. Silas stood and stretched his limbs.

"Some speech, huh?" Keck said.

"Yeah," Silas replied.

"He sure has it in for the Rebels," Keck went on. "I bet we go to battle real soon. With A.J. Smith's men coming here from Sherman's army, and with McClernand's men from Texas, we'll wipe every Reb clean out of this country."

Henry sat quietly in the grass. Silas noticed he was strangely calm.

"Keckley, you been home too long," Henry said. "We're on Southern turf, not the other way around. These boys consider our presence an invasion of their homeland. They fight like tigers. Even when we outnumber them two or three to one, they whip us." He reached for a twist of tobacco and put it thoughtfully in his pipe. "We'll never wipe this country clear of the people who farmed it and settled it. Especially with Napoleon leading us, eh, Silas?"

Silas chuckled. Napoleon was the nickname the regiment had given to General Banks, and the name stuck. A politician from Massachusetts with his eye set on the Presidency of the United States, Banks wasn't the most popular general in the Union army.

"Well," Keckley sighed, "there's no way Dick Taylor and his Johnnies are going to whip us—not with all the help we're getting."

"I wonder what Texas looks like," chubby, good-natured Joe spoke up. "I hear it's so wide, you can't tell where the sky ends and the land begins."

"We'll be finding out soon enough," Keckley answered.

Silas glanced at Henry. Henry said nothing but Silas knew Henry wasn't so sure any of them would ever see Texas—or home again, for that matter. A feeling of dread crept coldly into his heart. Silas shook it off.

"I'm starved," he said. "With McClernand here, we should have full rations today."

Silas was right. They received three days' full rations—dried, tinned beef and vegetables, which the men called "embalmed beef and desecrated vegetables," three cups of cornmeal, and all the coffee beans they wanted. Silas and Keckley went to their tent, crawled inside, and tediously began to open the tins of meat and vegetables with their bayonets.

"Put on a pot of water, will you, Keck?" Silas asked. "If we can soak these dried up things in water for a spell, they'll taste a lot better."

Keckley grabbed the small iron kettle they shared and left. He was back within minutes with fresh water from a nearby brook. Silas, who had finally succeeded in opening the cans, plopped the vegetables, a tightly caked mass of bright green, into the water.

"Hey, it's beginning to look like cabbage," Keckley said. "Want me to build a fire and heat it up?"

"Sounds good to me," Silas said with a shrug. He peered into the kettle and saw flecks of orange. "I think there's a piece or two of carrot in there, too."

Keckley laughed as he picked up the pot to take it outside. "Instant vegetables. Only in the army!"

"I like them better than those old slapjacks," Silas said. He took out paper and his pencil to write home to his family. He hadn't written for over two weeks.

23

He hoped they wouldn't be worried.

Suddenly Joe poked his head through the flap, nearly knocking Keckley over. Joe was clearly shaken and out of breath.

"What's the matter?" Silas asked.

"Smallpox!" Joe gasped, trying to catch his breath. "Ed, the drum major, has got it bad! Stay in your tents. We may have to be quarantined!" He closed the tent flap and was gone.

Silas put down his pencil. Smallpox. He'd rather face a hundred Rebs. At least with the Rebs he had a fighting chance.

Chapter Six

March 4, 1864

Silas fell into his blanket, exhausted, as the sun rose. They set up camp at Brashear, a small town on a large bay called Berwick, after marching for three days. They marched the last several miles during the night.

So far the smallpox epidemic hadn't spread to anyone else he knew. The Colonel kept the infected men quarantined. Joe told him last night that the drummer had died. Silas felt sorry for the poor wretch but didn't think too long about it. In war, men die. It was the only truth of which he was certain. A sad fact, but he accepted it. He had no choice but to accept it.

After a few hours of rest, Silas woke up, refreshed. The sun blazed its welcome heat over the brackish bay. Yellow rays danced on the dazzling blue water. Pelicans and egrets squawked as they flew gracefully overhead, searching for their breakfast.

"What a beautiful day," Silas said to Keckley, who was still curled up, unconscious, in his blanket. "I think I'll go fishing in the bay, Keck." Fish sounded good after a long voyage. No embalmed beef today, Silas thought thankfully.

Silas pulled on his brogans and reached for his haversack. Inside he found a roll of string and a few hooks he had brought from home. He put them in his pocket, picked up his rifle, and left quietly, not wanting to disturb Keckley.

Silas strode along the bank, filling his lungs with fresh air and enjoying the warmth of the sun. The wind had been cold on the water during the night. He passed a garrison of black troops. He had heard from Henry that Colonel Robinson's troop of negro soldiers were stationed here to build a fort for the Union. The soldiers worked hard, felling trees and splitting logs. Silas knew it was not an easy task, especially tackling a cypress tree. Some of them were as old as creation and as tough to cut through as a rock.

He spied a long, thinner branch dangling on a felled tree. A young soldier hacked mercilessly at the fallen trunk, trying to split it in two.

"Hey," Silas called. "Do you mind if I use a branch of this tree?"

The soldier looked up at Silas. Silas recognized him and smiled.

"Anthony."

"Hey," Anthony grinned, his eyes flashing. "You're the last person I expected to see, Silas. Except maybe my ma."

"We miss your cooking."

"That doesn't surprise me," Anthony replied as he swung the axe again. "I feel real bad that I couldn't say goodbye."

"That's all right," Silas said. "You joined up with Robinson, then?"

Anthony nodded. "What're you doin' up at this hour? Didn't you just get in at dawn? We heard you been travelin' three days."

"I'm going fishing. That's why I need a branch of this here tree."

"Bald cypress is the best kind. Help yourself. And keep on the lookout for Rebs. Word's out that a few gray-coats are in the area. They love to shoot at the color blue."

"Can I borrow your axe?"

Anthony handed it over, and with one whack Silas had his fishing pole.

"Thanks," Silas said. "Know any good spots?"

"Haven't had the time to check it out," Anthony replied. "Good luck."

"I'll bring you back a big one," Silas promised.

"Enjoy yourself while you got the time," Anthony said. "I heard this morning that Albert Lee's cavalry is due to arrive. When they call in the cavalry, you know we're headin' into some kind of storm."

"Yeah, one raining bullets."

"Watch your back, Silas."

"I will. You do the same."

Silas continued along the bank of Berwick Bay and selected a spot near some blackberry bushes. He checked the area carefully for snakes. Louisiana boasted over a dozen species, many of them poisonous. He wasn't taking any chances.

Satisfied, he dug in the moist earth until he found a large night crawler. He strung and baited his hook, then attached the string securely to his pole. He cast his line and waited patiently.

An hour passed without a nibble. Silas pulled a few berries off the bushes and ate them in silence. The day was warm and pleasant. He felt relaxed for the first time in weeks. The next hour passed slowly, still with-out success. Silas reached into the cool water and splashed it on his face. He tasted it with his tongue. It was fresh.

No wonder the fish weren't biting. The salt water fish that usually inhabited the bay couldn't handle the fresh water that spilled in when the Atchafalaya River rose. He pulled the line out of the water and headed back to camp.

He noticed on the walk back that their camp was surrounded by bayou, a small brackish tributary river engulfed in forest. He felt his back crawl. He didn't feel comfortable in the bayous. Alligators, snakes, bugs as big as his fist—all of them lay hidden in the dark swamps beyond. And Confederates. They were some-where in there, too. In the darkness that even the sun couldn't penetrate.

Silas's step quickened until he reached camp. Everyone was awake, some playing cards, others lying in the sun to soak up the warmth, and a few playing ball.

"A mail for you," Keckley said as Silas entered their tent.

Silas took the letter. "It's from my father," Silas said. He read it in silence as Keckley gathered together his clothes.

"I'm going to the water to wash," Keckley said. "You coming?"

"You go on. I want to write my father."

After Keckley had gone, Silas took out his pencil and a piece of paper emblazoned with Old Glory. He dated the top right corner, then wrote *Dear Father*. He always began his letters that way. Keckley once com-mented on its formality, but Silas ignored him. Keck's pa was just as formidable as Silas', but somehow their relationship was more casual. Silas couldn't bear to write anything but *Father*, though he easily called his mother "Ma." It didn't make sense, but Silas didn't care. There were a lot of things in life that didn't add up, but Silas figured he had to accept them just the same. This was one of those things.

March 4, 1864

Dear Father,

It was good to hear from you, and to learn the family and farm are well. Bayou Country, as you call it, is an exotic place. We have experienced a few skirmishes, but nothing to worry Ma about. Banks has ordered us to march toward Texas. I feel there will be a decisive battle soon. Don't worry about me.

Give my love to Ma and tell the rest of the family to please write me. I have not heard from Amanda in almost a year. Tell her I am appalled!

Affectionately,
Silas

Silas wrote his name neatly, with a small flourish at the end. He would mail it in the morning. He closed his eyes, thinking of Amanda. That sister of mine must have a beau, he thought as he drifted off. He was more exhausted than he had realized.

He awoke in twilight. Keckley knelt over him.

"Silas," he whispered. "Joe's sick. It's smallpox."

Chapter Seven

March 10, 1864

Silas stood steadily, his hand firmly holding the long stick they used for hitting, his eyes squinting in the bright sun. He tried to keep his eyes on Marcellus Conner, the pitcher and owner of the only real ball in camp.

Conner, whose aggressive nature overshadowed his slight build, hurled the ball. Silas swung, his stick nicking the end of the ball. It sailed past him into the weeds.

Keckley ran after the ball, searching the brush and cattails. "I can't find it!" he called.

The day was pleasantly warm. Silas looked at Keck. A few yards beyond the field where they played, the dark forest loomed ominously. Every time Silas looked at it, he felt uneasy. Keckley stood at its edge.

Dropping the stick, Silas walked over to join his friend. He parted the grass with his boot. Keckley continued searching with his hands.

"I'd be careful where I stuck my paws if I were you," Silas warned.

"Hey!" Conner shouted. "Hurry up! You had better find my ball!"

Silas started to answer, when he heard a shriek from Keck.

A large snake, dark brown with a sinister, triangular head, appeared from the vegetation, its fangs protruding from a pinkish-white mouth.

Cottonmouth, Silas thought, his heart lurching.

The snake lunged at Keckley, taking a bite at his brogan heel. Silas silently cursed the fact that he left his rifle with the rest, by home plate.

"Run, Keck!" he shouted. Its venom was as deadly as any bullet. He frantically searched for astone while Conner ran from the field with his rifle in his hands.

One blast and the snake lay dead. Keckley sank to the ground, staring at the still heap in front of him.

Silas walked over to his friend. "You have to be careful," he quietly admonished. He didn't say more, but he was worried. A couple of months at home had softened Keckley to a dangerous level. He hoped his friend learned from the experience. Silas vowed that he would never leave his rifle that far away again. He, too, had been foolishly secure. He looked into the forest.

What else was in there?

"Here's the ball," Conner's voice brought him back. "You're up, Silas."

The game continued until gray clouds rolled over and hid the sun. Suppertime approached and the men broke up, pairing off with mess partners. Silas scanned the groups, looking for Henry. Silas hadn't seen him all day.

"Have you seen Henry?" he asked Keck.

"No," Keck replied, still skittish from his tangle with the cottonmouth.

Silas ate with Keckley. Henry was nowhere in sight, and Joe was, the last they heard, worsening in his private battle with smallpox. Silas tried not to think about it as he devoured the corn bread he and Keckley made.

"This is really good," Silas said. The fresh bread was a welcome variation from tinned meat and vegetables, which they also ate.

Keckley nodded, his mouth full.

After their meal Silas picked up their tin plates and cups and the kettle.

"I'll wash the dishes tonight," he said. "You look a little peaked."

Keckley's lips cracked into a half smile. "I felt like an idiot, letting a little snake scare the stuffing out of me like that."

Cottonmouths weren't little snakes, and Silas had felt just as scared. But Silas said nothing.

The sky over the bay was bursting with colors ranging from daffodil to indigo. The clouds, hiding most of the sun, spilled over with purple that seemed to touch the bay in the distance. Birds of all kinds populated the water, fishing for their dinner.

Silas let his rifle drop and bent to fill the dirty dishes with water. He welcomed the gentle sound of waves lapping the shore—his only companion besides silence.

Silas finished his chore as dusk approached. He placed the plates and cups back in the kettle and reached for his rifle. As he bent to retrieve it, his eye caught a lonely figure sitting near a large cypress tree that faced the bay. Startled, he forced the feeling away when he recognized by the uniform that it was a Union man.

Slinging the Enfield over his shoulder, Silas made his way to the tree. He was almost upon the man before he realized in the coming darkness that it was Henry.

Silas stood before his friend as questions filled his mind. Where had he been? Why was he here alone?

One look at his friend and Silas knew something was terribly wrong.

They stood in the purple twilight in silence until Henry finally spoke.

"Joe died about an hour ago."

Silas felt a twinge of pain in his abdomen at the news. Poor Joe.

"I watched him die, Silas."

"I'm sorry, Henry."

Henry didn't reply. He stared at the lake.

Silas didn't know what to say. Joe was Henry's only friend besides Silas. It was hard watching friends die while being helpless to do anything about it. Silas felt equally helpless about words of comfort. He had none to give.

"You know," Henry spoke up, "you were right and I was wrong."

"Huh?"

"About the sunsets. They aren't all the same, are they?"

"No, Henry." Their conversation eons ago had been about sunrises, but Silas decided against mentioning that minor point.

"I'm tired of watching men die, Silas."

"So am I." A deafening silence followed. Slowly the last glimmer of light faded. "Let's get back," Silas suggested. "We don't want to be out here alone in the dark. The bushwhackers could be anywhere." Bushwhackers, or locals who took pot shots at straggling members of the Union army, turned up in the strangest places at any time of the day or night. The hair on Silas's neck stiffened as he thought of it.

Silas stood and waited for Henry to do the same. Together they walked, shadows against the endless ink that saturated the night sky, until they reached camp. After seeing Henry to his tent, Silas walked quietly to his. Keckley was already asleep.

Silas dropped onto his blanket and immediately fell into a deep sleep. He heard wolves howl in his dreams as he meandered through dark forests, watching for men in gray.

Suddenly he awoke with the breeze in his face. He was in a field, and Keckley snored by his side. A stab of fear welled up inside, until he focused.

A fierce wind had blown away their tent.

CHAPTER EIGHT

March 16, 1864

Silas sat before the campfire, the chill of the night air penetrating the marrow of his bones. Almost a week had passed since Joe's death. The dull ache had diminished with long marches and hard work. The past week had filled their days with endless marching, foraging, and, under orders to do so, marauding. The vestiges of their travel were marred with desolation.

Silas looked at his dusty shoes. The filthy roads made the entire regiment grimy with dust. He didn't recognize anyone and figured he was probably as indistinguishable as the rest. He reclined against his knapsack and stared into the endless black above him. His feet hurt.

How many miles had they marched in the last few days? They had averaged thirteen or fourteen miles a day since they left Berwick. He remembered passing through a town called Franklin and following the river to New Iberia, where they now rested. Here the bayous gave away their domain to prairie. Silas thought how much it looked like home and felt an emptiness he'd never known before. He missed his parents, his brothers and sisters, his cousins, and his friends. He missed the farm and all the animals he used to grumble about having to tend. He wondered how big Rosie's calf had grown by now. He thought of it romping with its spindly legs on the prairie, nipping at his mother's tail and testing her patience as she grazed.

When the war started he had yearned to travel, see new places, experience the thrill of battles and other dangers. Well, he'd seen enough and experienced enough. Two years ago he sat at home and thought of faraway lands. Now he sat in a faraway land and thought of home. He smiled at the irony.

In the dog tent, Keckley lay awake as Silas entered.

"I hear we're on the march again tomorrow, first thing," Keckley said.

"That's what I hear, too," Silas answered.

"I been looking on the map," Keck said. "The next town is St. Martinsville. It's not too far."

"Good."

"But Conner says we're marching to Vermillionville. It's at least eighteen miles away. I told him there's no way we'd go that far in a day when we don't have to. Conner says he heard Sarge receiving the order from Lieutenant Dran."

"Banks is in a hurry to get to Texas," Silas said.

"I learned from Martin that farther north the bayous and forests take over again." Keckley said. Silas grimaced. He felt comfortable here, where prairie grass was the only thing between him and the stars. But they had their orders. They would go northwest where the forests, the Confederates, and probably death as well, awaited.

Chapter Nine

March 20, 1864

Silas marched, footsore and heavy with fatigue. The weight of the gear on his back grew heavier with each mile. His regiment tightly surrounded him, and scores of soldiers from other regiments making up the Nineteenth Corps followed for miles. They had long passed Vermillionville. It had been an eventful stay as Confederate skirmishers fired into them three miles from their destination. One man in the infantry was killed—Silas hadn't known him, much to his relief.

Today they were heading toward Bayou Begg, near Washington town. Silas decided every state must have a town called Washington. North and South alike idolized the man, believing that somewhere in the great beyond the first President sympathized with their opposing points of view.

As they passed Opelousas, a light rain began to fall. It picked up wind as they reached camp. Silas and Keckley quickly put up their tent as the drizzle turned into a downpour.

"Cross," Silas heard his name and turned to see Sergeant Jones. He didn't salute—one didn't have to salute a sergeant or call him "sir,"—but Silas respected the dark-haired, heavily bearded leader as much as he did any general.

"You're on picket," Sarge said abruptly and walked away into the gray.

Silas sighed. He didn't want sentry duty tonight in the rain. Every muscle in his body ached. But orders were orders. He reached into his knapsack and pulled out his black rubber rain poncho. He hurriedly slipped it over his head, replaced his kepi, grabbed his rifle, and left without a word.

The sentry post stood near a hut occupied by a family of free blacks. They didn't venture out in the rain to welcome him, but a small boy poked his head through the open doorway from time to time. Silas smiled and waved. The child shyly ducked inside each time. Silas had joined the army for children like him. He couldn't picture living without freedom to do as he wanted. His spirits rose as the rain tapered off.

The three long hours passed at last. Silas moved stiffly from his position when Conner came to relieve him at nine.

"We're getting a new commander for our corps," Conner said.

News traveled fast, even among the constantly growing troops.

"Who?" Silas asked, stifling a yawn.

"General Ransom."

"Too bad he's not replacing Banks," Silas muttered.

"No one ever replaces that dunderhead. He's still in charge of the whole thing." Conner shrugged.

As more soldiers joined them, a new corp commander took the lead if he outranked their current one. A.J.

Smith and his men were due to join them in Alexandria. Silas wondered if Smith would assume command once they hooked up with him. He hoped as much.

"What else did those ears of yours capture?" Silas asked, grinning. Back in Iowa, Conner would be famous as the town gossip. He overheard everything. Trouble was, he told it all, too. He'd probably tell a Johnnie if he were willing to listen.

"There's a bunch of plantations nearby. Some scouts found one a couple of miles from here, full of cows and sheep and a shed full of sugar." Conner smiled slyly. "So, we'll have full bellies tomorrow."

"That's good news, Conner." Silas liked the thought of eating fresh meat again. And having dessert! How long had it been since he ate something sweet?

Living off the land was the best way for the Union soldiers. But the Confederates, soldiers and private citizens alike, preferred killing their livestock and burning their crops to letting them fall into Union hands. He hoped no one had seen the scouts, or tomorrow they would be too late.

CHAPTER TEN

March 27, 1864

Alexandria, a beautiful plantation town on the Red River, bulged at its unexpected surge of inhabitants. The Federals lay idle after having gorged themselves on the food they foraged from the nearby plantations, including the one Conner had mentioned.

Silas lay in his tent feeling content, no longer sore after marching and living off meager rations for weeks. Keckley had made a blackberry cobbler with the sugar from the plantation and the bounty of blackberries they picked from bushes that surrounded the area. Silas felt full for the first time since he left home. Home didn't seem as far away on a full stomach.

A.J. Smith and some of his men were leaving for the front today, near Shreveport. Two more of his divisions remained. Silas had caught a glimpse of the bespectacled, gray-whiskered commander from Pennsylvania, and was impressed. Smith was a fighter. They had a chance after all.

"Keckley, why don't we go into town?" Silas suggested.

Keckley looked up from a Waverly he'd already read twice. "Why?"

"It looks like something worth seeing, that's why."

Silas and Keckley invited Henry, but he declined. He still seemed troubled, a fact that disturbed Silas. Henry had to snap out of it.

Conner was asleep. Martin, Applegate, and McCane were busy playing poker.

"I guess it's just us, Silas," Keckley said.

They walked, excited as schoolchildren on holiday, past residences that proudly displayed their finery. Pillars and porticos flanked the fine antebellum mansions, each one grander than the others as Silas and Keck passed by. The scent of jasmine and honeysuckle sweetened the air. Bees hummed gently in the blossoms.

"It's like another world," Silas said. "A fairy tale land."

Keckley laughed. "These bayou people sure don't seem to be hurtin' to me."

As Keckley spoke Silas noticed a woman on the portico. She was young and lovely, her dark hair pulled sharply back, her worn crepe dress blue as a robin's egg. Her dark eyes shot sparks, and her expression was anything but genteel.

"Evening," Silas said cheerfully, as he tipped his kepi.

She didn't speak or move. She stood like a statue, her eyes spewing venom. Silas and Keckley walked on. Silas could feel her glare as they passed, but he refused to look. He understood her hatred. Probably someone she loved—a brother or a sweetheart—was more than likely dead on a nearby battlefield. He wished it didn't have to be so. But it was, and neither he nor she could do a thing about it.

Her eyes haunted him, just the same.

CHAPTER ELEVEN

April 6, 1864

Silas sat in front of his dog tent near Pleasant Hill, trying to spot the sun in the dense pine woods where they camped. After three days in Alexandria, the phalanx of men marched north and west through Natchitoches, a quaint town of French origin on the Red, and Grand Ecore. After the village of Grand Ecore, they entered hilly terrain and thick forests. The cumbersome roads slowed their march. To make matters worse, Banks ordered seven hundred wagons of provisions and medical supplies for his vast army. He bragged that his troops would sacrifice nothing. But Napoleon Banks had forgotten that someone had to cart the monstrosities through the forests. Silas rolled his eyes. Thousands of men were deep in enemy country, trusting their lives to an empty-headed politician who pretended to be a commander. No one found it humorous.

One bright thought entered Silas's head. Henry was doing better. They talked the day after Silas and Keckley toured Alexandria. Silas told Henry about the girl with daggers in her eyes.

Henry had smiled, to Silas's relief.

"And you expected her to invite you in for a mint julep, I suppose?" he had quipped.

They laughed and Silas felt better. Henry was going to be all right.

Silas rubbed the dust from his brogans. Yesterday he thought he would choke on the dust. Whoever thought wars were glamorous? This war was one long two-step with only dirt and bullets between the blue and the gray. He thought again of the young woman on the portico. He hadn't seen a lady for a long time. The trollops in New Orleans didn't count, and he had kept his distance from them. The girl in Alexandria had definitely stirred something within him. She was no doubt good and decent, brought up by parents that planned her future carefully—just as his parents had done. If the war hadn't come, he would probably be courting a girl in Iowa—someone young and beautiful like the girl on the porch. If only the war hadn't come.

But it had come.

Silas pushed the dreams aside. Someday he would go home, and life would begin again. At least he hoped it would. He leaned against the tent and closed his eyes.

In his mind he saw the girl again. He remembered the Confederate Henry had killed a moment before the soldier would have slain Silas. He shuddered as he remembered the same look in the Reb's eyes.

He hated being here. Eyes were hidden everywhere, watching him.

CHAPTER TWELVE

April 8, 1864 – morning

The sound of reveille blasted through the pines that shrouded Silas and his regiment from the rest of the world. The soft glow of sunlight filtered through as Silas rubbed his eyes. He prodded Keckley, who lay snoring beside him in the tent.

"C'mon Keck," he said as he left the welcomed warmth of his blanket. A battle was imminent today. News from the front arrived. Word quickly spread through camp last night that Kirby Smith and Dick Taylor with their Confederates held the line at Sabine Crossroads near Mansfield, a few miles beyond the forest where the Union slept. Yesterday Banks' seven hundred wagons had nearly choked all communication between Albert Lee's cavalry and the rest of the Union army. Silas reflected again on the incompetency of his commander. The Rebs could have annihilated the cavalry because of those cumbersome wagons blocking the way of both aid and escape. Silas shook his head.

He felt uneasy in the darkness of the woods. He hoped the front was open. Trees had a funny notion of suddenly turning into men with gray coats and guns.

After a quick, cold breakfast of hardtack, the forest came alive with thousands of men in navy blue sack coats, their gleaming bayonets affixed to their rifles. They marched in orderly fashion to the beating of the drums, some singing "Glory Hallelujah," others thoughtfully silent. Ahead a dozen columns in the distance, the flag unfurled, its thirty-five stars and thirteen stripes riding on the gentle breeze. Silas caught a glimpse of Henry in the row ahead. Henry turned and looked at him. Silas smiled.

Henry's mouth, masked because of a full beard that now graced his chin, cracked a smile in reply. He lifted three fingers to his kepi and saluted his friend. Silas saluted back.

Silas wished he could talk to Henry to reassure himself that Henry was back to normal. Henry's head, however, was every bit as cool in battle as Silas'. Keckley was the one to worry about. Silas craned his neck and strained his eyes to find Keckley. Failing to catch sight of him, Silas hoped luck would be on Keck's side today. He hoped it would be so for all of them.

The pop and crackle of gunfire sounded faintly in the distance. The men marched on, hearing the boom of artillery and the cries of the wounded as they drew nearer. The talk between rows grew as the light beyond the forest brightened. Someone said there were 25,000 Confederates waiting to fight them.

Silas, knowing they still outnumbered the Rebs with A.J. Smith's men and the Corps d'Afrique, reflected on Henry's words to Keckley: *They fight like tigers. Even when we outnumber them two to one, they whip us.*

Silas blinked as shells exploded in the distance, sending men sprawling in every direction. The heat of the blast reached Silas in seconds. As the smoke cleared Silas glimpsed a field, followed by a low hill directly ahead. It was dark with men. Beyond it Silas noticed another patch of forest by the crossroads, Sabine Crossroads, and in those trees he saw scores of grays and butternuts. Thousands of them. Silas felt his body grow numb.

Hold on, he thought. Easy, Silas. He gripped his rifle. He had sixty rounds of ammunition. Every bullet had to be carefully used. He breathed deeply as he stepped onward with the surrounding infantry. Be calm, Silas. Be calm.

He wished a safe return for all his friends and others in the regiment, but now he could only look out for himself. He crouched low as the whiz of bullets hummed in his ears. He heard the fierce shriek of the Rebel yell and it sent a shiver through him. Henry's words echoed in his mind: *Tigers. We've invaded their land and they resent it.*

Silas greeted the open field with caution. He saw the Corps d'Afrique, Robinson's men, on his left flank. Anthony was probably with them. Good luck, he thought. Dick Taylor took white prisoners but never black ones. Even if they surrendered they were ordered to their feet and shot. Silas hoped Robinson's men would fight like tigers, equal to their foe.

The Rebels whooped and ran toward them, shooting their muskets with uncanny accuracy.

Screams of pain shot through the air, muffled by the sounds of heavy cannon and gunfire. Silas tried to avoid looking at the bodies of the dead that lay in grisly heaps, some beginning to bloat from the sun. He shot, reloaded, and shot again, each time taking careful aim. He remembered his folly during the last skirmish. He had pitied the enemy and given one of them another chance; and it almost cost him his life. He liked being far enough away so he couldn't see their faces. He couldn't stand to look at them. They were too much like his own.

Silas's heart pumped wildly. Blood flowed inside like a torrential rain. The battle reminded him of a storm, with the artillery and gunfire thundering, the bullets and the glistening bayonets flashing like lightning.

From the corner of his eye, Silas watched a butternut soldier, his feet bare and his rifle empty, give a Union man a taste of his bayonet as the Federal soldier shot him. Both fell to the ground, motionless and twisted around one another.

"Forward, men! Forward!" A lean, swarthy man in blue on an ebony stallion shouted. It was Colonel Slack. Silas forged ahead, his heart pounding, his eyes searching, his rifle ready.

Another shell exploded in the distance, sending men flying and others running. The acrid odor nearly choked the men nearby. Silas ducked to avoid fragments. They could cut a man in two as easily as any minie ball.

Through the dense, suffocating smoke Silas saw figures running toward him. He couldn't make out the color of their uniforms. He raised his rifle. They shrieked and leaped at him and the scores of other soldiers in blue. Rebels. Silas shot. The other rifles fired simultaneously. The men dropped. Some lay silent, others cried out in pain. Silas hurriedly reloaded and walked on, refusing to look down. He couldn't bear it if he looked down.

The line of blue marched on into the woods. Silas noticed some of the men in gray retreating. Good, he thought. Perhaps this fight would end.

He heard a trumpet echo eerily from the forest and realized he was wrong. A cloud of gray burst from the trees behind the crossroads, some on horses but most on foot. They ran swiftly, their faces contorted. The spine-tingling howl that sounded half-human, half-animal filled the Yankees' ears and seized them with horror. The Rebel yell was unnerving, which was exactly why the Johnnies used it.

The line of Union soldiers fell back to prepare for the sudden rally from the men in gray. Both sides collided, and it seemed to Silas that the ground beneath him shook. The whirlwind of men fought savagely, hitting one another with the butts of their rifles and their fists. Many didn't take the time to reload their muskets, so eager were they to fight each other.

In the confusion Silas saw Colonel Slack on foot, his dead horse lying a few feet away.

"Retreat!" he screamed.

Retreat? No, Silas thought. Not yet.

"Retreat!" The words sank into the ears and minds of the men as the bugle sounded. The soldiers around Silas obediently withdrew.

Silas reluctantly followed orders. If they turned and ran, General Taylor would chase them down.

He hated being on the defensive. Perhaps Banks knew something they didn't. Maybe Taylor really did have 25,000 men. Or maybe more. As Silas thought, his steps grew longer and quicker.

The soldiers in gray followed them through the smoke, screeching and shooting. Silas reloaded, ran a few yards, then turned and shot. He ran on, unable to reload while fleeing, glancing back as often as he could.

He saw Henry several paces behind him. He, too, paused to shoot at a Confederate in the artillery-induced miasma.

Silas stopped. He watched as a man on a horse charged toward his friend. Henry shot and frantically jumped out of the horse's path. Henry's intended target, a finely dressed officer with a dark beard and flamboyant moustache, returned a shot as he flew past. Henry fell to the ground. Silas felt his stomach tighten and his knees go weak.

Silas sank to the ground, the smoke thick around him, the bullets popping in the distance accompanied by cries and screams. Silas crawled to Henry. He would carry him all the way to Iowa if he had to.

"Henry," Silas whispered as he reached the man who had saved his life in the bayou. He pulled Henry by the arms and struggled to move him. Henry's chest was covered with blood. The ground was saturated with a puddle of red. Silas abandoned the hope of moving him and crouched beside his friend, heartsick.

"You'll be all right," Silas said, knowing it was a lie. He lay low in the smoke as more men in gray passed. In their haste to overtake the Yankee hordes, they overlooked the two figures lying quietly in the haze.

"Henry!" Silas looked into his friend's face. "Say something. Anything!"

Henry said nothing.

Silas stood slowly, blinking back tears, dejectedly accepting what he already knew but hadn't wanted to believe.

Henry was dead.

He saved my life, but I didn't save his, Silas thought bitterly. He felt a lone tear slide down his cheek.

A volley from Confederate artillery burst nearby, and Silas leaped to his feet.

He grabbed Henry's rifle and ran, trying to erase

the ghastly memory from his mind. He had to reach his regiment—fast. Or he was dead, too.

Silas reached the forest where the Union army had fled, straining his ears for sounds of battle. He followed the noise, grateful at last for the trees that hid him from Confederate eyes. Slowly he made his way among the conifers. Dozens of wagons, the mules having been cut loose, cluttered the forest like skeletons. All the supplies had been stripped clean. He hoped his men had the supplies, but suspected otherwise. Near one of the wagons he found Conner, lying peacefully as though he were asleep, in the woods. His rifle and haversack were gone. Just below Conner's right ear Silas found the bullet hole.

Conner and Henry. And Joe, too. Silas felt a sickness deep in his gut that swelled until it reached his heart.

Where was Keckley? He thought of Keck lying in the field somewhere. Please, don't let it be, Silas thought. He continued his journey, dodging behind the massive trees whenever he heard voices or footsteps. He dared not peek to see who passed. He was sure the men weren't Union soldiers.

He had trudged on for nearly an hour when he caught a glimpse of blue through the woods. Relief flooded every fiber of his body. The Confederates had gone. For now. Silas knew they would be back.

"Who's there?" a sharp voice demanded as Silas approached.

"Silas Cross. I'm one of you."

A portly man emerged from the trees, his brass buttons ready to pop from the strain of keeping his uniform together. His black hair and beard bore heavy streaks of gray.

"What's your regiment, son?"

"28th Iowa."

"They're a few miles up the road. If you can call it a road." He gave a gruff laugh, then turned serious. "Better hightail it right quick back to your regiment. Banks has ordered the hastiest retreat in the history of the world. He knows the graybacks are hot on our heels."

"But," Silas said, trying to stay calm, "we have dead and wounded out there. We need to bury the dead and treat the others."

The soldier grunted. "The medical supplies are already on the way back to Grand Ecore. We couldn't treat the wounded if we wanted to. Banks says to leave 'em all. If they can't walk, they're out of luck."

Silas felt his back arch at the grim news, his eyes ablaze with anger and tears he wouldn't allow to surface. He walked past the sentry and into the woods, loathing Banks more ardently than he could ever hate any Rebel.

He felt the late afternoon sun on his back as it seeped through the trees. He couldn't look at it. He would avoid the sunset tonight at all costs.

He wouldn't be reminded of Henry, who lay on the battlefield, denied a decent burial.

CHAPTER THIRTEEN

April 8, 1864 – evening

Silas stole into camp just as the sky began to relinquish the sun. Men huddled in mess groups around hastily built fires, eating with their rifles at easy reach. Silas looked away. His mess group was no more as of today.

Silas stepped through the groups of tired, dirty men. He wondered how many wounds the Rebels created today. Fragments of memory flashed in his mind as he searched the massive crowd for Keckley. The blasts of artillery. The smoke. Henry.

No, he thought forcibly. I've got to find Keck.

"Cross!" a group of six from the 28th Iowa called his name in unison. Martin, a tall redhead with freckles and Irish wit that surfaced daily except during battle, held up a plate.

Silas walked over to their fire and sat down. Weariness overtook him as suddenly and heavily as though a sutler's cart had fallen on his back. He closed his eyes and for a few moments thought he would never be able to open them again.

"You look like the very devil," Martin said as he handed him his own plate.

Silas took it, grateful for his comrade's hospitality.

"I must," Silas replied.

The men ate voraciously, without conversation, as the food disappeared. Silas finished quickly, partly because of his sudden hunger, partly because of his need to find Keckley.

Sergeant Jones appeared in the distance, pausing by each mess group. Silas was sure he was giving the orders to move. When he reached Silas and his mess, the sergeant's blue eyes were somber and tired.

"Finish up, men. We have orders from General Banks to move tonight towards Grand Ecore. Immediately." He tipped his cap and stepped away. "We'll get past Pleasant Hill tonight, anyway."

"Sarge," Silas said quietly, "is Keckley around?"

Sergeant Jones stopped as if frozen. It seemed an eternity to Silas before he turned back to face the campfire.

The steely blue eyes bored into Silas'.

"He's in the tent," Sarge said bluntly as he moved on.

Silas understood Sarge didn't have time for inquiries about one's lost friends. Thousands were lost today, that Silas knew for sure. But Keck was alive! In the tent. Silas knew the meaning behind that title. The only tent standing besides the commanders' was the surgeon's. He grimaced as he stood.

"Thanks, Martin," Silas said as he handed the tall Iowan the tin plate.

"Sure," Martin replied. He smiled. Silas managed a wry one in return. There isn't much to smile about, he thought as he walked off.

The surgeon's tent was on the east end of camp, a large, ominous makeshift hospital of canvas. Outside, men lay bleeding and moaning on the ground. Silas lifted the flap and recoiled from the stench of rotted flesh and blood that rushed to overtake him. Groans of the wounded echoed from every direction, tugging heavily at his already morose spirit.

A uniformed orderly with a blood-spattered apron hurried from cot to cot. He must be getting them ready to move out, too, Silas thought. He hoped Keckley would be able to go.

Two soldiers from the Corps d'Afrique met Silas as he stepped inside. Silas recognized one of them as Anthony and felt an immediate surge of relief. Someone else he knew had survived the pandemonium of the day.

"You looking for your friend Keckley?" Anthony asked.

Silas nodded.

"He's over there, in the corner." Anthony pointed a finger in the increasing dark. "He caught some shell fragments. He's gonna be all right, though. He was far enough away when the shell exploded."

"That's the best news I've heard today," Silas breathed. "Thanks."

Anthony and his partner opened the flap. A cool breeze filtered through, mingling with the putrid scent around them. "We got to get back to our regiment. Robinson says we're moving out tonight."

"So I hear," Silas answered. He waved as the two men left. As his eyes grew accustomed to the approaching darkness, he saw his friend. Keckley lay still on one of dozens of cots, all filled with suffering men. A red-stained bandage covered the crown of his head.

"Keckley," Silas touched him gingerly on the shoulder. If he were asleep, Silas didn't want to wake him.

Keckley opened his eyes.

"Silas," he croaked. "You're alive. I was so worried when I didn't see you."

"Do you hurt much?" Silas asked. "Anthony said you got hit with some shrapnel."

"It don't hurt. Not really. Anthony—he was really something. When I got hit, I just lay there for the longest while. Rebels kept passing me right and left. Anthony and another fella, they found me and helped me get back. I'd still be lying there if they hadn't helped me out. I couldn't think. It was like I was in a dream."

"Nightmare is a better word," Silas said sullenly.

"Yeah," Keckley agreed. He tried to move and winced. Silas noticed red seeping through the thin blanket on his legs.

"You hurt in the leg, Keck?" Silas asked, worried. Amputations ran rampant in the Union Army. Any wound of depth got the saw—and whatever limbto which the injury attached itself went with it.

"Yeah, but Anthony poured some brandy on it after the doc pulled out the shrapnel." Keckley gave a short, weak laugh. He looked up at Silas. "Don't worry, they aren't taking my leg off."

"Surely not," Silas agreed. He ran his fingers through his tousled black hair. He felt tired.

"You hear news of anyone we know?" Keckley's voice came out of the dim light of lanterns and candles.

Silas stared at the ground. He dreaded the task of telling him.

"Did Henry make it back?"

Silas slowly shook his head.

"Conner?"

Silas shook his head again.

Silence engulfed the air between them. Together

they sat without a word until the blood spattered orderly came to Silas.

"We could use your help, Corporal. We're moving out now. I guess the Rebs are nipping at our heels. General Banks wants as much distance between our armies as possible."

Silas nodded and stood wearily. A long march after today's battle was pure punishment. And probably more fighting tomorrow. More punishment.

He patted Keckley's arm. "See you, Keck," he said.

Silas carried men to the few wagons salvaged by the Union. The rest would have to walk. He knew Keckley's pain was intense as he helped place him in the overcrowded cart. The wagon, filled to capacity, lumbered off in the darkness.

"Where will they go?" Silas asked.

"New Orleans, probably," the orderly said. "There's a home for wounded soldiers there."

CHAPTER FOURTEEN

April 9, 1864

Silas awoke in the gray pre-dawn and pulled out his pocket watch. It was six a.m. They ended up a few miles from Pleasant Hill, twelve miles from Grand Ecore.

He had slept fitfully. He barely slept whenever he found himself in the midst of battle. He patted his rifle. He would need more ammunition today.

As the camp came to life, he thought of Henry and how much he would miss him. Conner too. He hoped Keckley would make it to New Orleans all right.

I'm the only one left, he thought guiltily and wondered why.

They slowly ate hardtack in silence. At eight a.m. they met A.J. Smith's command.

"The Johnnies are skirmishing with the pickets at all posts," Colonel Slack informed the regiment. "Let's annihilate them, men!"

Silas fell in line and began the march into battle. Skirmishers hid in the trees, taking pot shots at the mass of soldiers.

They're buying time, Silas thought. The full force will hit us soon.

The morning passed slowly, uneasily. The sun climbed high over the hills when the men heard the dreaded Rebel yell.

Pleasant Hill clamored with the sound of musket and cannon fire. Soldiers sprang to life. Union men shouted and yelled to drown the sound of the Rebel shrieks. Perched near a large red pine, Silas saw the hordes of men in gray and fired his rifle. He loaded again, pushing the bullet down with his ramrod, and coolly fired again.

A.J. Smith and his men fought with ferocity. Silas felt they were closest in disposition to the Confederates. Silas felt relieved that he was on their side. He aimed at a Rebel and fired again. When the smoke cleared the man had fallen to the ground.

A soldier screamed and ran towards Silas, his eyes blazing with anger. Shots rang through the battle site, and the man fell. Silas huddled behind his tree and reloaded. Ironically, now he liked the trees.

The two sides fought all afternoon. Silas could tell the Union was gaining the advantage. Once he caught a glimpse of A.J. Smith on horseback. The middle-aged Pennsylvanian rode calmly among them.

"Hold the line, boys," he said. "We'll send them running today."

Silas felt secure among the hardened soldiers. Within two hours the enemy was gone. Silas looked at the battlefield littered with bodies of men and horses.

"Prisoners!" a yell shot through the troops. "We got us a heap of 'em!"

"How many?" Silas asked.

"Hundreds of 'em. Don't know the exact count yet," a young, scrawny boy—for he couldn't have been more than fourteen—answered. His black eyes glowed with excitement, like smoldering coals.

"What'll we do with all those Rebs?" another soldier asked.

Silas silently watched the commotion. He didn't know these men and he didn't care. He would never know them. It was the path of least resistance—and of least pain.

CHAPTER FIFTEEN

April 11, 1864

Silas sat alone in his dog tent at Grand Ecore. He felt rested and his stomach was comfortably full. A herd of unlucky cattle had found their way to the Union lines. Silas hadn't tasted fresh beef since they raided the plantations.

At Grand Ecore two letters caught up with him, one from his mother and another from his sister, Amanda. Hearing from them brought him the comfort he desperately needed. Someday, if he survived this catastrophic war, he would go home to them. Someday.

From his tent he could see the docks where boats brought men daily to save them from Rebel clutches. All around the Red River, Silas saw the dark blue of Union soldiers.

In the distance he heard the crackle of musketry and the boom of cannon. The boat was coming. The Confederates were no doubt firing upon it. He realized the sound of gunfire no longer startled him. The insight left him oddly cold.

The sound of falling timber grasped his attention. General Franklin had ordered the building of breastworks to halt the Confederate army in their tracks.

"They're coming, no doubt about it," General Franklin announced earlier that day. "And you men are to finish this work as soon as possible. You'll hold this line if the Rebs have to walk over your dead bodies."

Yes, sir, Silas thought. Taylor, the Rebel general, would probably go below them anyway. He'll blockade the river, Silas mused. He had done it before. Wily as a fox, Taylor loved to outsmart the Federals.

The cavalry stayed in nearby Natchitoches. Word spread that Taylor lived there. Silas knew the town was doomed. Albert Lee's cavalry was determined to burn it to the ground.

If the Rebels go to Natchitoches first, Silas thought, they'll get a warm reception.

Silas lay on his blanket and tried to clear his mind. He would go on picket duty in a few hours. He tried not to think of the question that gnawed at him since the day of their last skirmish. Why, after winning the battle of Pleasant Hill, had they retreated? Why were Kirby Smith and Taylor chasing them when it should be the other way around? He knew the answer.

Banks.

Napoleon Banks had foolishly ordered the retreat. Still, the question ate away at his insides.

He trusted his life to a poor commander, as had so many others. They now languished in Rebel prison camps or slept in shallow graves.

Will my luck run out, too? he thought uneasily.

CHAPTER SIXTEEN

April 19, 1864

The alarm rang through camp in the dark.

"To arms!" men shouted as bugles blared.

Silas jumped out of his blanket and hastily dressed. He pulled on his brogans and grabbed his rifle and ammunition.

They waited breathlessly in hordes, watching the shadowy horizon for the first sign of gray uniforms.

As dawn broke, Colonel Slack brought the order from General Franklin. The enemy would not fight today. False alarm.

"Draw three days' rations and be ready to march at an hour's notice," the lean, serious officer said.

"Do we have three days' rations?" Silas wondered aloud.

"I doubt it," a soldier at his side said. "That idiot Banks gave it all to the Johnnies along with all our medical supplies."

"A.J. Smith and his men will get us food," another soldier added. "He should be the one in command."

Silas silently agreed with them. They'd be in Texas by now had Smith been in command. Or anyone else but Banks.

His stomach growled, tight with hunger. He thought of the food he and Keckley cooked together and hoped Keckley was alive and able to walk by now.

Chapter Seventeen

April 24, 1864

Silas marched swiftly in line with the endless phalanx of men. A column of blue stretched in front of him as far as he could see. Behind him it was the same.

The wooded countryside greeted them with silence broken only with the sound of tramping boots. The sky grew dark in the distance. Night was coming and they were still far from their goal of Alexandria. Silas's thoughts wandered to yesterday's skirmishing that commenced at Cane River. With a vengeance, Dick Taylor's army singled out A.J. Smith's men, who took up the rear of the army. After a hard fight, the battle ended at sundown. Silas was weary of fighting.

As they marched in the dusk, fires lit their way. The Union soldiers burned every building in sight.

"Did you hear about Natchitoches?" a young soldier ahead of him asked another comrade.

"No," came the reply.

"The cavalry burned it. But General Taylor, as soon as he learned about it, tore through the country 'til he reached his hometown. Put all the fires out, he did."

His companion scoffed. "Too bad A.J. Smith wasn't there. He would've burned it to the ground."

In the corner of his mind, Silas heard Henry.

We're on their turf and they resent it. We'll never wipe this country clear of the ones who farmed it and settled it. Especially with Napoleon leading us, eh, Silas?

Silas looked up into a small patch of fiery orange sky, the last shred of light surrounded by darkness. It reminded him of a battlefield ablaze with cannon fire.

"That's right, Henry," Silas whispered.

In the rear a song commenced to a familiar tune. Soon it spread throughout the ranks:

In eighteen hundred and sixty one
We all skedaddled to Washington.
In eighteen hundred and sixty four,
We all skedaddled to Grand Ecore.
Napoleon P. Banks!

Silas found himself singing along with them. Strangely, his heart felt lighter mocking his plight.

Chapter Eighteen

May 1, 1864

Silas reported for sentry duty at dawn, exhausted from extensive marching. So far the retreat to Alexandria remained quiet. Boats and trains regularly brought bounties of corn and cotton from deep within the Southern borders. Silas eagerly ate the corn every day for almost a week without tiring of it. Another comforting reminder of home.

Everyday he heard gunfire from upriver. Occasionally a wounded Union man or a Rebel prisoner entered camp to be treated or questioned before being shipped elsewhere. The last prisoner, proudly wearing a worn gray coat, had displayed open defiance. Silas worried that the young Rebel might not survive the night after his loathsome words.

"We hate you all," he had hissed. "And we'll die before we let you Yankee scum pollute our land with your presence!"

He then spit on the Union officer who questioned him. At mess that night Silas heard talk of an "accident" that would befall the captured Rebel.

"No," one of the men in Silas's regiment said. "Let the prison break him."

"Prison's too good for that grayback," a nameless Union man replied.

Somehow, General Franklin learned of the plot and increased guards on the lone prisoner. This morning the captured Johnnie left for a makeshift Union prison up the Mississippi. Even in war there were rules about prisoners. Shooting each other in battle was one thing. Murdering a prisoner in cold blood was another. Sometimes Silas failed to understand the difference, especially when news leaked to them about the Confederates gunning down unarmed Union soldiers. General Franklin, however, dismissed it as propaganda. And rules were rules.

Silas shrugged and watched the horizon, his stomach in knots and his joints aching. His heart leaped, beating solidly when he caught sight of figures, shadows against the morning sky. Rebel vedettes. He fired his rifle into the air, and they disappeared.

Sergeant Jones ran to his side. "What is it?" he asked calmly.

"Rebel vedettes, Sarge. I saw about a half dozen of them."

The leader nodded slowly. Silas felt his nerves tighten. Vedettes always appeared before a battle. Dick Taylor, determined general that he was, couldn't be far behind. Now they knew where the Union camped. Another battle. Silas began to feel ill.

He noticed Sarge looking at him with watchful eyes. But Sarge said nothing.

Silas rubbed the back of his neck. "I'm all right. Just tired like everybody else."

"Good. Applegate relieves you at nine. I'll report the vedettes." Sarge left as quickly as he came and Silas was alone again.

Within minutes mounted cavalrymen tore past Silas's post. Several more minutes passed before Silas heard the crackle of gunfire.

Applegate, another young, swarthy member of the 28th Iowa, showed up at nine.

"You look kinda peaked," he told Silas. "Are you sick?"

Silas clutched his stomach as the ground below him seemed to spin out of control.

"I'm . . . fine," he insisted as the nausea swam within him.

"Better get to your tent and sleep it off," the soldier said as Silas left him.

Silas walked slowly toward camp. He shook with chills and aches as he fell into his tent. It was undoubtedly the ague.

A Confederate bullet would have brought welcome relief.

CHAPTER NINETEEN

May 7, 1864

Silas lay huddled in his tent, healing from the sickness that plagued him all week. He decided it had been a good week to be ill. Rations were once again in short supply. In the past few days all he had managed to consume was beef crackers and some blackberry tea.

He looked at his pocket watch. It was seven a.m.

Martin and Applegate pulled back the flap from Silas's quarters and peeked in.

"You look better today, Silas," Applegate commented.

"I feel better," Silas said quietly.

"We're moving out today," Martin said. "Hope you're in the mood for a long march."

Silas nodded. He wasn't in the mood to do anything, but he decided moving was better than being left behind for the enemy. He stood in his long undergarments, his blanket falling to the earth.

"How soon?" Silas asked.

"Real soon," Applegate answered. "Now, in fact."

Silas dressed and folded his belongings in his knapsack. Martin and Applegate helped him by striking the tent. Together they settled in with the others as they prepared to move out.

Armed with sixty rounds of ammunition each, the mass of soldiers fell in line and began their journey.

Silas felt stronger as he marched beside Martin and Applegate. All he needed was a good meal. He wondered when, or if, he would get one of those again.

Lieutenant Dran rode on a chestnut horse to their line.

"Martin," he said, "we need you to ride ahead with a few other volunteers from our regiment. More Rebel skirmishers. Take care of them."

"Yes, sir," Martin saluted. He turned to Applegate. "Come with me," he said.

"I'll go, too," Silas said.

"You're still not well," Martin replied. "You shouldn't go."

"Don't tell me what I shouldn't do, Private Martin," Silas said calmly. He had never pulled rank before. Martin was his friend and the best shot in Company C. But Silas outranked him, and didn't appreciate Martin telling him he couldn't go.

Martin's eyebrow lifted slightly. Silas knew Martin was surprised by his words.

"Corporal, sir," Martin said seriously, "you are not well. You'll be nothing but a target."

"Silas is a good shot," Applegate argued. "He can handle himself."

Martin said nothing. He stared at Silas. Silas knew Martin was right. He shouldn't go. The marching was hard enough after a week of sickness.

"You fellas be careful," Silas admonished.

Silas watched silently as his two comrades ran ahead to mount horses. He hoped they would return.

They marched until they reached a large bayou.

"Pontoons needed!" General Franklin called.

Silas watched as dozens of engineers spent the next few hours putting together the collapsible bridge they needed to cross the water. Some bayous were shallow enough, but some were deceptively, and dangerously, deep. General Franklin had given the order. An intelligent man and veteran fighter, Franklin's word always sufficed.

The wagons rolled across the wooden planks to the other side of the silent, coffee-colored water. In the distance Silas heard gunshots as he crossed the bridge.

Silhouettes of men appeared on the horizon to Silas's left. He recognized the deep blue coats and relaxed.

A few miles beyond the bayou, the army made camp. Silas put up his tent. Once inside he stretched out on his blanket. He began to drift off to sleep when Applegate entered.

"Mind if I come in?" he asked.

Silas sat up and rubbed his eyes. "Hello," he said. "Is everyone back?"

Applegate grinned. "Yeah. We didn't lose a single man. We scattered the skirmishers. And," Silas could tell he was ready to spill big news, "we got ourselves a Rebel colonel!"

"You took him prisoner?"

"No, we shot him. He was sneaking up on us and Martin saw him. He was planning to pick us off one by one. But we got him instead." His eyes gleamed proudly.

Silas remained silent. It was certainly better to have killed one of the enemy to save a dozen of his own regiment. But, like Henry, he was tired of the killing. He wanted to go home.

He thought of the colonel alone against so many Union soldiers. When did valor go too far? When did it turn to foolishness? When did it turn to suicide? He dared not mention these thoughts aloud. Applegate would think him a coward, and Silas was no coward. He refused to be reckless, though. No medal was worth being a fool.

CHAPTER TWENTY

May 13, 1864

"Silas!" Silas looked up from his dinner of crackers and coffee to see who called him. He saw Martin running toward him.

"Did you hear? The gunboats all made it downriver! We'll be moving out in a few days."

"I'm glad they made it," Silas replied as he bit on a cracker, his main sustenance for the last few weeks. The Red River, being too low for navigation, had left the Union gunboats perilously isolated. Banks had gone upriver in an attempt to solve the problem. Silas was amazed that Banks actually succeeded in solving one.

The Union cavalry reported the enemy in strong force within a day's march. Skirmishes were common every day in the front and rear of the army. As usual, A.J. Smith's division held the rear. Silas readily saw Franklin's wisdom in placing them there. No Rebs would take the army from behind. The entire corps of soldiers idolized Smith. And they detested Banks.

"Where are we headed?" Silas asked.

"The Atchafalaya River, then on to the Mississippi," Martin replied. "With your permission, corporal, I gotta tell Applegate. See you."

Silas waved casually and took a drink of his coffee. The Mississippi. The Father of Waters. He had seen it before, many times. He hoped to see it again.

Chapter Twenty-One

May 21, 1864

The mighty Mississippi coursed like a large, pulsating vein in the earth. Silas found himself smiling as he heard a roar of joy from the troops. They were as glad to see the great river as he was. Of course, the joy was mingled with a bittersweet goodbye to Smith and his troops. Ships waited to take them up to Vicksburg, then to northern Mississippi to fight Nathan Bedford Forrest. The Red River Seige was over. A dismal failure.

"Where will we go now?" Silas heard a young private ask.

Lieutenant Dran, on horseback, looked down at the youth. "We'll go on down to New Orleans," he said. "We'll receive orders once we get there." He smiled, but Silas saw no humor in the curved lips. "Don't worry, boys," he said, "there's plenty more fight left in us, and U.S. Grant won't let it go to waste!"

"Are we staying here, sir?" Silas asked.

"No, we're marching on to Morganza," the officer replied. "But not until nightfall. You have a few hours to rest, write home, bathe, do whatever you like. But beware of the skirmishers. The sentry saw more vedettes this morning. Bushwhackers might be nearby, too."

"How far is Morganza?" Silas asked in a low voice to Martin, who stood beside him.

"Far enough," Martin murmured. "I'm tired of marching. We must have traversed the entire state of Louisiana."

Silas chuckled softly. Martin, no doubt, was right about that fact.

A large mail caught up with the regiment, and Silas was thrilled to find two letters from home. He hadn't received mail for weeks. Father and John again. His younger brother William enclosed a sentence along with John's letter. *Sorry I ain't ritten,* he penned incorrectly. *I ben busy.*

Silas snorted. Busy? "That's a good one, Will," he said aloud. "Wait 'til you hear what I've been doing."

The sound of laughter and splashing interrupted his reading. He looked up to see hordes of men in the river, swimming and bathing. Silas knew the army was long overdue for a good time. He pulled off his shirt and trousers and jumped in with them.

The water was deep and cold. The dust and heat washed off easily, chasing away mosquitoes and taking along the memories of the past few weeks. He climbed up the bank and leaped in again and again. He was careful not to collide with anyone. The group of bathers wisely kept close to shore, as the current could sweep the exhausted army away. Silas eyed the hundreds of closely set heads and shoulders and grinned. *Even the Mississippi isn't big enough for the Union Army today,* he thought wryly.

After an hour of swimming, Silas dried off and put on his uniform. The sun didn't seem as hot now. He stretched out on his blanket and continued reading his letters in the sun. A droplet of water from the river ran down his cheek. He touched it. Days ago the same drop was most likely traveling by Iowa. He closed his eyes and fell asleep, dreaming of home.

CHAPTER TWENTY-TWO

May 30, 1864

Silas stood at attention in the rain. Inspection was a daily ritual now, besides roll call three times a day. Thank goodness there's no drilling, Silas thought. Only the new recruits were required to drill.

He looked around him. The army was rapidly diminishing in size. Regiments left daily on steamers for other parts of the country. Word spread that the 24th and 28th Iowa would soon board the steamers to fight elsewhere. Silas eagerly anticipated traveling to another area and fighting under a different commander. News flowed about Grant, their Vicksburg general, now commanding the entire Union Army. Grant was back east in Virginia.

"Fall in!" came the order from Colonel Slack. Silas obediently fell into line. They would march again today with two days' rations and sixty rounds of ammunition. Silas didn't enjoy marching in the rain and worried that the wet would make them ill.

The army marched slowly in the muck and mud surrounding the Atchafalaya River. Silas noticed they walked parallel to the water, obviously following it. They would eventually reach New Orleans if they didn't board a ship soon, but the backtracking to confuse the Confederates irritated him.

Upriver Silas heard the boom of cannon and the crackle of gunfire. The Rebels continually fired on the steamers that left for Vicksburg every morning.

I think I'd rather take my chances on land, Silas decided.

The army marched for hours. In mid-afternoon a scout discovered four skiffs hastily hidden on the bank.

"Rebel skiffs," Lieutenant Dran said. "Destroy them."

Silas helped pile the boats in a heap. Sergeant Jones lit the gathered reeds under them. Soon the blaze rose high toward the sultry sun. When they were certain the boats were destroyed, the soldiers marched on.

By midnight they had marched twenty-two miles. Footsore and with aching shoulders, Silas was ready to rest. He was sure the entire corps felt the same.

"We'll camp here," Lieutenant Dran said as he slid off his horse. Crickets chirped in the distance.

"You heard him, men," Sergeant Jones called out. "Put up the tents. Eat your rations quickly, without fires. We don't know where . . . "

A sudden burst of gunfire tore through the troops. Sergeant Jones gasped and fell forcefully to the ground, grasping the newly made hole in his left arm.

Silas, along with the rest of the troops, quickly situated himself behind the wagons and artillery. Their dark uniforms blended well with the night. The firing continued into the troops. Silas heard more cries and knew more men had been wounded.

In the scant moonlight Silas couldn't make out any silhouettes of gray. In a distant clump of trees, he saw the flash of bullets.

"There!" he whispered emphatically to Martin. "They're holed up in that bit of woods."

"I know what'll send them flying," Martin said grimly. He nodded toward the artillerymen.

The artillerymen grabbed the cannon and struggled to turn it to aiming position

Lieutenant Dran busily wrapped a tourniquet over Sarge's arm. He looked at James Satchell, the gunner, and nodded.

Satchell hurried to the cannon, a Napoleon, capable of firing a shell for over a mile. He motioned for the other artillerymen to join him as he quickly calculated the distance and wind. He aimed the cannon toward the woods.

"Ready," he said as two soldiers loaded the gun with a flannel bag of gunpowder, a disk of wood, and a twelve pound cannonball. The first soldier, called the Number One Man, shoved the ammunition into the barrel with the rammer. The second soldier inserted a metal pick at the back of the Napoleon to puncture the bag of gunpowder so it would ignite. Immediately he plugged the hole with a vent pick and friction primer, which was attached to the lanyard. Without air the gunpowder would not explode. The third soldier held the handle of the lanyard, ready for the gunner to give the order.

With a cool eye on their target, the soldiers backed away from the cannon and waited.

"Fire!"

The third soldier pulled the lanyard. A huge blast roared from the cannon and splintered the trees that housed the Confederate skirmishers. Silas heard cries of anguish, followed by silence.

"As I was saying," Sergeant Jones said resolutely, grimacing with pain, "we'll camp here for tonight."

A few men laughed and began setting up their tents.

Silas sat motionless on the ground, listening to the talk and laughter of those around him. He watched as the smoke from the cannon curled into the sky.

He was so tired of it all.

Everywhere they went the Rebels pursued, taking pieces of the unit each time. He watched the men set up camp as though nothing unusual had happened. A stretcher came for Sergeant Jones. Lieutenant Dran stood nearby, watching as Sarge was carried away.

"He'll lose his arm, won't he, sir?" Silas asked.

Lieutenant Dran turned, his face stricken, his coat covered with blood. The two leaders were the best of friends. Like Keckley and Henry had been to him.

Lieutenant Dran nodded and followed the stretcher into the darkness.

CHAPTER TWENTY-THREE

June 8, 1864

Silas finished picket duty at nine a.m. Already the sun beat down, oppressively hot. After a nap, he would take a swim.

He spied the sutler's cart on his way into camp. He reached into his pocket, jingling the loose coins. He was ready to buy today, no matter what the price.

"What do you have?" Silas asked.

The sutler scowled. "Almost nothing! Where were you last few hours, boy?"

"I was on picket duty."

"Oh. Well, then." The heavy-set man with thin gray hair softened. "Some of your men saw my cart and went crazy. They overturned it and stole most of my goods. What they didn't take, they wrecked. What do they think I am, a Confederate?" He cracked a sly smile. "Your colonel had them arrested, though. Serves 'em right, the fools."

Silas said nothing, his eyes fixed on the cart. Though the marauders were fools, he felt a flash of anger in their defense.

"I have a few apples left. They got a little bruised when the cart overturned, but they're good," the sutler pitched.

"No, thanks," Silas said and walked on.

Silas was pleased to see supplies had arrived earlier that morning. He figured hunger and monotony were the culprits that drove the soldiers to folly with the sutler. Boredom often caused as much trouble for the army as the battles.

After a breakfast of bacon and corn bread, Silas curled up and fell asleep. He awoke to the crack of thunder, mistaking it for skirmishers. The steady patter of rain sent him back to sleep. When he woke again the sun was shining, and steam lifted from the ground.

Sweat trickled down his back.

That's it, he thought. I'm going swimming.

Silas made his way slowly to the banks of the bayou, his rifle in hand. The muddy ground stuck to his feet like tar and was just as black. A group of soldiers screeched and played in the bayou, some swinging from a rope tied to a large red cypress, others splashing in the dark waters.

Silas stripped off his uniform and jumped in the water, pleasantly surprised at its coolness. It was deeper than it appeared.

"Over here, Cross!" Martin cried from the opposite bank. "Try the rope!"

Silas swam, his brown eyes taking in the simple beauty of the bayou. Trees surrounded it on both sides. Branches filled with leaves and blossoms reached into the waters. Above, the trees sheltered the swimmers from the sun. Except for the occasional sound of a bird, the only sounds were the exuberant bathers. But, Silas thought, that's noise enough.

Reaching the bank, Silas climbed out and waited his turn in line for the rope. He laughed as Martin fell headfirst, howling like a scared dog. The gigantic splash soaked everyone in line.

"Watch it, Martin!" Applegate called. "My eardrums are shattered, thanks to your big mouth!" He grabbed the rope and swung out to the middle of the bayou, dropping silently into the water. Two more waited ahead of Silas.

Applegate rose from the water with a shriek. Martin laughed at him, stepping out onto the bank of the opposite shore.

"What's the matter, Applegate?" he jeered. "Get your hearing back?"

Silas laughed along with the rest but stopped when he saw the terror in Applegate's eyes.

"Help me, somebody!" Applegate screeched.

A collective gasp resounded from the horrified crowd as all eyes fell on the large bull alligator that glided silently towards Applegate. Its red, primeval eyes stared coldly at its target. Everyone rushed out of the water. Only Applegate remained, struggling to reach shore as the alligator drew closer, quietly stalking his prey.

Silas remembered his rifle on the opposite shore.

"Martin!" Silas shouted. "My Enfield is on the bank over there! Get it!"

Martin dashed to the spot where the rifle lay and grabbed it. He returned to the water's edge and took careful aim.

Silas heard the shot as Applegate struggled in the shallows, the water hugging his chest. Martin fired again, and the alligator rolled belly up, mere inches from its intended victim.

For a long moment no one spoke. One by one the men left.

Applegate, visibly shaken, stepped on the shore.

"Thanks, Martin," he managed.

"These are dangerous waters," Martin called. "Good thing Silas thought to bring his rifle."

"Yeah, good thing," Applegate echoed.

Silas dived in the water and swam quickly to the other side. He picked up his clothes, slung his rifle over his bare back, and headed toward camp as Martin waited for Applegate to summon his courage to swim again.

Silas arrived at camp alone. He entered his tent and, wanting to busy himself so he wouldn't be forced to think of what had almost happened, began writing to Will. His busy brother. After the salutation, however, his pencil remained poised over the paper.

What would he say? He put down the pencil.

Martin appeared in the open entrance. He grinned impishly.

"Hey," he said, "I brought my rifle. Wanna go swimming again?"

Silas thought for a moment. He tossed the writing paper aside and reached for his Enfield.

"Sure," he said. "Let's go."

CHAPTER TWENTY-FOUR

June 20, 1864

Silas was eager to arrive in New Orleans. Along with Applegate, Martin, and three others, Silas had procured a twenty-four hour pass.

The soldiers perspired heavily in the intense, wet heat. They had walked the six miles from Carrollton, where the rest of their regiment camped, in order to save money for souvenirs. Silas felt richer than the others. He received ninety-six dollars, six months pay, rather than the two months the rest picked up. He had not drawn salary the last two times. He remained taciturn about the cash. He knew the others would be on him like an owl on a rodent if they knew.

They roamed aimlessly through the French Quarter, meandering in and out of shops, eyeing the pretty ladies who refused to look at them in return. They ate ice cream on Bourbon Street for twenty cents a bowl.

"Any of you know where the Soldier's Home is?" Silas asked as he finished the last of his delectable treat.

"No," Martin said, hastily shoveling the ice cream in his mouth before it melted.

"Why do you want to go there?" Applegate asked.

"I want to see if Keckley is there. I heard he might be," Silas answered.

McCane put down his empty bowl. "I'm not sure of the exact street, but I think it's somewhere in the French Quarter."

"Of course, he could be wrong!" Martin laughed.

Silas stood and replaced his wooden chair by the round glass table.

"I'll see you in a couple of hours. Where would you like to meet?" Silas asked.

They settled on the riverfront a few blocks south. Silas walked off.

He roamed Royal and Chartres Streets, and finding no building for Union soldiers, began to walk the docks. He found an old Creole, his hair coarse and gray, his face a testament of many years spent at sea. He was selling fish on the wharf.

Silas towered over the man. "Sir," he asked, "do you know where the Soldier's Home is? The one for Federal men?"

The old man pointed a crooked finger to the western horizon and spoke in a language Silas couldn't understand. Silas nodded politely, his eyes exposing his confusion.

The man gestured down the street. "Yankee, go that way. Red house."

"Thank you," Silas said, tipping his cap. He hurried down Decatur Street in the direction the fishmonger had pointed. After wandering a half hour more, he found it at last, about a mile from where they had eaten ice cream.

Silas entered the once grand, now shabby, red brick edifice with wrought iron fence and widow's walk.

Ceiling fans mitigated the intense afternoon heat. Silas glanced at his watch. It was three o'clock.

He removed his kepi and smoothed his shiny hair. With his hat in hand, he entered what he assumed was the office, hoping to find someone. Anyone.

He stood in the doorway and gave a sweeping search of the room. It was empty.

"Hello! Is anyone there?" Silas called.

A middle-aged man dressed in a colonel's uniform entered from a back room.

"Can I do something for you?" he asked nonchalantly.

"Yes, sir." Silas saluted. I'm looking for someone who may be staying here. A private named Thomas Keckley. He was wounded a while back."

"Oh, yes. Private Keckley. You'll find him in the kitchen."

Silas was not surprised by the answer. "Could you point me in the right direction, sir?" he asked.

"Down the hall. Turn right."

"Thank you, sir." He saluted and left the room.

Silas walked down the hall, soon aware of the fragrance of food. He found the kitchen easily.

Keckley stood over a large stove, stirring a steaming pot. He was thin, but Silas noticed with relief that he was standing on both legs.

"Keck."

The tall, blond Iowan turned abruptly, as if he were startled. His eyes widened.

"Silas Cross! Well, I'll be . . ."

Silas walked toward his friend with his hand outstretched. Keckley limped, but a broad grin stretched across his face as he clasped Silas's hand in his own.

"What are you doing here?" Keckley asked.

"I heard you might be here. I have a pass. But only for today."

"One day? You mean you can't stay?" Keck's grin faded.

"We're moving out at four a.m."

"Oh."

Silas turned his attention to the large pot. "I see your talents haven't been wasted."

Keckley's eyes shone with pride. "You've got to taste this, Silas. It's a new dish a Creole taught me to make."

Silas stepped to the stove and lifted the lid. Steam rushed upward to the ceiling. A strong, pungent smell filled the air.

"What is it?" Silas asked.

"Gumbo," Keckley replied as he ladled a dish of it. "Sit down here and try it."

Silas sat down at the closest table, staring at the bowl Keckley placed in front of him. Translucent white meat, rice, and strange green pods floated in deep red broth.

He picked up a spoon. "Something in there is staring at me," he said.

"Aw, just try it. I promise nothing bad is hiding in there. But it's hot, so be careful."

Silas scooped up a spoonful and blew away the steam. He took a long look at Keck, then obligingly sampled the concoction. The spices and heat brought tears to his eyes.

"Like it?" Keckley asked with eager eyes.

Silas nodded. "This is wonderful," he said, wiping his eyes with the back of his hand.

Keckley smiled with satisfaction. "It's good stuff. I knew you'd like it."

"So, you're the cook here," Silas said.

Keck nodded. "I'm no good at combat with this busted leg. But the soldiers like me. They say I'm the best cook around."

"Well, I certainly agree with that," Silas agreed. "You'll be staying here, then."

"Yeah. What about you?"

"I don't know where we're going," Silas admitted. "Some say we're going up the Mississippi to fight. Some say Banks is going to march on Mobile. Others say we're going east. Who knows? Orders change with the weather. We may stay here, marching from one end of the state to the other." Silas finished his meal.

"Want some more?" Keckley offered.

"No, thanks. I'd like some water, though." He removed his pocket watch and looked at the time.

Three-fifteen. He had to meet the others soon. Too soon.

"While you're here, you should visit a shop on Decatur," Keckley said as he set a cup on the table. "They etch your portrait on a piece of glass for real cheap. Good likeness, too."

"Thanks, maybe I will." Silas lifted the cup and took a long drink.

The doors opened and soldiers filed in.

"Here they come," Keckley sighed.

Silas took Keckley's hand and shook it. "I guess this is it. I'm glad I saw you again."

Sadness unfurled on Keckley's face. He couldn't look Silas in the eye. It was an awkward moment. Silas turned to go.

"Wait," Keck said. He reached into a barrel and pulled out a small loaf of bread. "Take this. It's a lot lighter than that old hardtack."

"Thanks." Silas took the bread gingerly. After handling hard tack for so long, he was afraid regular bread would break in his hands.

Keckley stared at the floor. "See you back home, then."

"Yeah. Definitely."

"Write me when you get settled. I promise to write back."

"I will," Silas replied. "Goodbye, Keck."

"Goodbye, Silas. Take care."

Silas left. Once outside he broke the bread in half and shoved the separate pieces in his pockets.

He hated goodbyes.

CHAPTER TWENTY-FIVE

June 24, 1864

Silas sat on the bank and finished the last of Keckley's bread. Outside the rain had finally stopped.

Kennerville, a village ten miles from New Orleans, was situated on the left bank of the Mississippi River. They were to remain there for several days.

For the first time since Sabine Crossroads, Silas decided to watch the sunset. He knew it would be worth seeing tonight with all the scattered clouds.

He listened to laughter from the tents. He heard the soft sound of a distant fiddle. He couldn't make out the tune.

Martin and Applegate had invited him for a game of poker, but Silas declined. Somehow they learned about his ninety-six dollars, now dwindled to eighty-two.

Earlier in the day the mail had reached them. Their first mail in over a week. Silas had waited, trying to mask his excitement, as the names were called. At last he heard his name, but to his dismay he received only a newspaper. No letters.

It doesn't matter, he thought as the sun, a sliver of gold on the horizon, dipped into the river. I know they haven't forgotten me.

Still, it hurt.

Today was his twentieth birthday.

CHAPTER TWENTY-SIX

July 14, 1864

Silas softly whistled the song *Do They Miss Me At Home?* as he wiped the shaving cream residue from his face. After roll call and inspection, he planned to swim in the Mississippi. The recent rain had considerably cooled Louisiana. The relief lifted the men's spirits.

Silas was glad for another reason, too. They were leaving soon for Washington, D.C. Some of the Iowa and Wisconsin regiments had already gone. All would fight under Philip Sheridan, the cavalry commander. Grant's orders. Once again Silas felt the thrill of adventure and the excitement of visiting a faraway place.

"You thinking about our little voyage, Cross?" Applegate's drawl accompanied the sudden glow of sunlight as he pulled back the tent flap.

"Isn't everyone?" Silas asked as he secured the top button of his jacket.

"I hope you don't get seasick."

"I hope you don't," Silas quipped in reply. A steamer would ferry them around the Florida Keys and north to Virginia. "My only worry is the Confederate warships."

Applegate snorted. "They're too busy blasting everyone out of the water on the Mississippi. The

Atlantic's a lot bigger. We'll be harder to find."

"Yeah." Silas pulled on one brogan, then the other. "Ready for roll call."

Dew clung to the grasses as Silas and Applegate waded through to where the men assembled. Sergeant Jones, now without his left arm, and Lieutenant Dran stood before Silas's regiment. One by one the lieutenant called their names. One by one they responded.

"We have a new shipment of Springfield rifles," Lieutenant Dran announced. "Take your Enfields to Colonel Slack's tent and turn them in. You'll get new ones today. Inspection will begin at nine a.m.."

One by one the soldiers lay down their old rifles in a pile outside the colonel's quarters. As Lieutenant Dran watched, each man took his turn reaching into the large wooden crate that housed the new rifles. When Silas reached the pile, he gently placed his Enfield rifle on top of the rest. A heaviness tugged at him.

It's like saying goodbye to another old friend, he thought.

He drew the new Springfield, its metal barrel shining in the weakened sun, its wooden butt a rich brown.

Lieutenant Dran also drew one of the rifles from the pile.

"Watch closely," he said to the men. "I'll show you how to load it. It's a muzzle-loader, like the Enfield, but lighter to carry and more accurate. Takes half the time to clean, too." He pulled open the paper cartridge with his teeth. He smiled. "You still get the lovely taste of gunpowder."

The soldiers laughed.

"Pour the powder down the barrel, push the bullet in with your thumb," Lieutenant Dran went on as he demonstrated. He pulled out the ramrod and inserted it in the barrel. "Push it all down there real good, then pull back on the hammer and place the percussion cap like so." He held up the rifle. "Then just aim and shoot. I want to see every man load his rifle."

Silas watched as the men obediently loaded the new rifles. Silas took a paper cartridge filled with gunpowder and the bullet and ripped it open. He followed the lieutenant's directions and soon had the Springfield loaded.

"Good, men. Fine," Lieutenant Dran said. "You're dismissed."

Silas started for his tent with the Springfield in his hands. He turned one last time to see the Enfields in the pile. He looked again at his new rifle.

He hoped it would serve him well.

CHAPTER TWENTY-SEVEN

July 21, 1864

Silas stood at the dock in the darkness, along with seventy-five men, the only ones left of his regiment. He heard footsteps in the distance. Two more regiments would board the steamer with them.

He felt tired and hungry. Rations again fell to short supply. For one week they existed on hardtack and water. Yesterday Silas used some of his money to go into town and buy cabbage and potatoes. What he didn't eat he shared with Martin and Applegate. What money they had left from their day in New Orleans they had lost gaming. Silas couldn't let them starve.

He looked at his watch. It was nearly midnight. A gentle breeze stroked his face. The steamer, a large black and white vessel, waited like a sentinel on the silent banks of the Mississippi. A newer model, it came equipped with screw propellers to the rear instead of paddle wheels. In the moonlight Silas read its name, in white block letters, on the port bow.

Drago.

General Grover gave the order to board. He would be on the ship with them. General Emory, another commander of Iowans, was awaiting them in Virginia. The

28th Iowa walked up the wooden gangplank, followed by the other units. Silas remembered some of them from the battle near Mansfield. They were New Yorkers.

The ship filled quickly with soldiers. Silas secured a place on deck. He avoided going into the hold—and would continue to shun it unless absolutely necessary. He didn't like dark, cramped quarters.

Martin eased through the crowd and stopped at Silas's side.

"How many do you think there are?" he asked.

Silas shrugged. "Three hundred, maybe. It's going to be a squeeze."

Martin sighed. He looked tired.

"I've never slept standing up before," he said wearily.

"Horses do it all the time," Silas answered. "It'll be all right. Let's hope the water holds out."

Martin turned to face the lights of New Orleans. "Don't remind me."

General Grover boarded last. He returned the salute from the officials on the docks.

Silas and Martin watched as the gangplank slid from the ship. The whistle sounded. Slowly, the steamer eased downriver. Soon the lights of New Orleans disappeared.

Silas pulled away from the deck. He sat down and removed his knapsack and Springfield. He leaned up against the wall.

"Martin, you look as tired as I feel. Why don't you get some sleep?" he asked.

"I don't like this," Martin said uneasily, gripping the rail.

"You'll feel better after you get some sleep," Silas said.

"We're sitting ducks."

"The Rebels can't see us in the dark," Silas protested. "Come over here and get some rest."

Martin appeared reluctant as he sat down against the wall. Silas closed his eyes.

A sudden lurch woke him a few hours later. The sky slowly surrendered its darkness for the soft light of dawn. Confusion swept through the ranks.

"What's happened?" Silas asked Martin, who stood nervously at the rail.

Martin didn't answer, his eyes fixed on the sea.

Silas rose and darted to his friend's side. He saw they were positioned at the Mississippi delta. Ahead lay the Gulf of Mexico, its endless waters looking gray in the slow birth of light.

"We're not moving," Silas said to Martin.

"We're stuck," Martin said, his anger rising. "We're sixty miles from New Orleans, trapped on a sandbar! The Johnnies'll use us for target practice."

Chapter Twenty-Eight

July 22, 1864

"Don't worry, men," General Grover said, attempting to calm the troubled troops. "The ship's captain has signalled shore. From there we've telegraphed New Orleans. Three tugs are on the way. We'll get off this thing in a few hours."

The hours passed slowly as the sun poured its merciless heat upon the crowded soldiers.

The men fell sullenly silent, the only sound being the screech of a gull overhead. The smell of salt and fish was oppressive in the intense heat. Silas looked over the rail into the endless waters of the Gulf of Mexico. He stared with longing at the water, then walked away. The temptation to jump was too great.

Silas heard the cries for water around noon. They were denied.

Martin had gone below to find Applegate. Silas preferred waiting on deck. The heat in the hold was unbearable. At least up here he felt an occasional breeze.

Three tugs appeared in the distance on the widened mouth of the river. Slowly, they made their way to the grounded ship. Silas watched with interest as tanned men worked hastily, tying ropes as thick as cables to the ship.

He listened to the shouts of soldiers and sailors as the tugs pulled.

The ship did not move.

Silas wiped the sweat from his brow. After an hour of continuous failed attempts, the tugs left, churning back up the Mississippi.

We're stuck here forever, Silas thought with dread.

CHAPTER TWENTY-NINE

July 24, 1864

Silas woke, glad to see gray clouds overhead. The air was thick with the smell of rain. At least today they wouldn't suffer from the heat. Day Three on the bar had begun.

A light drizzle kissed the cheeks and foreheads of the masses on deck. Most of the soldiers stood with their faces inclined, their tongues protruding to catch some of the scant moisture. Silas watched them with pity. Everyone was suffering.

General Grover guarded the water supply with ardent determination. Silas understood the need for caution. Once the water was gone, there was no more. Already two full days were lost. But the men, including Silas, needed the water. Desperately. Silas swallowed with difficulty. His throat felt so dry.

The men cheered when water in tin cups was distributed.

"Three swallows," Lieutenant Dran commanded.

Silas eagerly took the cup, passed to him by an unfamiliar face. He's probably a New Yorker, Silas guessed as he downed the tepid liquid. Regiments were supposed to remain as a unit, but in the confusion a chaotic mix of troops resulted. Silas wiped his lips after the third swallow and passed the cup.

He heard another rousing cheer and peered over the rail. He joined in the yelling when he saw boats on the horizon. He counted them.

"Seven! No, eight!" he shouted. Seven tugs and a riverboat drifted closer, their puffs of smoke and steam swirling toward the clouds.

General Grover appeared on deck.

"Men," he said, "we are getting off this bar. When the riverboat pulls up beside us, you are to board her in an orderly fashion. Get your gear and fall in."

Silas watched as the boat pulled up expertly beside them. Two planks, one on the starboard bow and the other on the stern, slid across and were secured by the crew.

Silas crossed the gangplank. For nearly an hour man after man filed past. The planks withdrew.

Two hundred and forty exhausted men watched on deck as the seven tugboats pulled the grounded steamer.

Silas watched with interest. He hoped the boats succeeded. If not, what then?

Suddenly he heard the boom of artillery. Several yards from the steamer a cannon ball exploded into the gulf.

"Rebs!" he heard someone shout.

Silas ran to the rail. He saw them, a dozen gray, unmistakable figures with one cannon on the shore. They were approximately a mile away. He watched as they loaded again.

Silas felt his heart pound as the second shell came their way. It, too, fell into the water and detonated, soaking every man on the port bow.

If they don't get this boat free, Silas thought with dread, we are sunk. Literally sunk. He grimaced as he watched the Rebs on shore load another ball into the monstrous gun.

"The Drago! She's moving!"

Silas peered over the rail. He heard a gravelly, scratching sound as the boat glided across the sand and into the water. The soldiers yelled with both joy and trepidation.

"Hurry, men!" General Grover shouted. "Back to the Drago! Double quick!!"

The men ran across the hastily placed planks and onto the other ship, as another round was fired into the air. Sailors on the tugs fired their rifles toward shore. Silas knew the Rebs were too far away for rifles to be of any use.

The shell exploded, miraculously missing again. The *Drago* eased into the Gulf of Mexico and headed out to sea. The soldiers cheered, elated.

They were on their way at last.

CHAPTER THIRTY

July 29, 1864

"So, that's where the whole thing started," Silas mused aloud as they passed Fort Sumter and Charleston, South Carolina. The sun sparkled on the Atlantic like thousands of dancing diamonds. Silas couldn't help but feel impressed with the beauty of the South. Her cities, those in Louisiana and those he passed on the sea, like Savannah and Charleston, were proud and fine.

If Martin and Applegate feel better, he thought, they might want to see this. He decided to brave the hold, which the soldiers dubbed "the hole," to check on them.

He found them where he'd left them since they escaped the sandbar. The two Iowans lay moaning, pale and miserable from seasickness.

Silas knelt beside them. "Are either of you on the mend?"

Martin didn't move or speak.

"No," Applegate whispered.

"We've just passed Charleston," Silas said. "We expect to arrive at Fortress Monroe tomorrow night. Weather providing, of course. But it's beautiful out there now. No high waves like yesterday."

His friends didn't answer. They weren't the only ones afflicted. Over half the troops suffered, from mild stomach aches to violent illness. Silas didn't feel well either, but he managed to ignore it. He anxiously looked forward to docking in Virginia tomorrow. He had seen enough of the high seas.

Silas emerged once again on deck. He breathed deeply, filling his lungs with the salty air. Charleston lay behind them now.

He took his old place at the rail.

Next stop was Chesapeake Bay.

CHAPTER THIRTY-ONE

August 1, 1864

The *Drago* traveled up the Potomac toward Washington. Silas had finally talked Applegate into joining him on deck. Martin remained below.

Virginia was every bit as fascinating as Louisiana, yet the two states differed geographically as much as North and South did on politics. Trees lined the river, which was smaller than the Mississippi but equally majestic. Silas listened to the ubiquitous chatter of birds and squirrels hidden in the various branches of maple, hickory, sycamore, and oak trees.

"Isn't it better up here?" Silas asked.

Applegate smiled weakly. "Yeah. But then we ain't out to sea anymore."

Through the trees on Silas's left, an expansive white mansion emerged. Silas recognized it immediately.

Mount Vernon.

One by one the soldiers removed their hats.

They arrived in Alexandria, Virginia, soon after and disembarked the ship. Applegate left Silas to search for Martin. Silas preferred to stay alone. He didn't want to become close to them like he had to Keckley. Or Henry.

He carried his rifle and pack, which felt considerably lighter, and walked through the town. Another Alexandria. It felt good to be on land again.

Fireflies danced in the distance, lighting up briefly in the dusk. The damp heat seemed as thick in the air as it had in Louisiana. Funny how the two Alexandrias were so distant from one another, and yet so similar.

Alexandria, like her sister city in bayou country, emitted an atmosphere of aristocracy. Every building, even the modest homes of brick or clapboard, exuded elegance. Silas ambled through, admiring.

A reminder of better times, Silas thought. And, hopefully, a herald of better times to come.

At midnight Silas found himself on the ferry to take him and the rest of the troops to Washington. They arrived at the capital at one in the morning.

They camped that night at the Baltimore Depot.

CHAPTER THIRTY-TWO

August 18, 1864

The 28th Iowa and scores of other soldiers came upon General Ord's Army of the James in a driving rain. A heavy skirmish with Jubal Early's Confederates had just ended near Winchester, with the usual heavy Union losses. Silas hoped the battle was over for a while. He was tired from the long march over the Blue Ridge Mountains. He had never seen mountains before. The Blue Ridges were garden-like, filled with exotic birds and swathed with trees. Beautiful but deceptive. They were monstrosities to cross.

"Don't worry about missing the action, boys," General Grover said. "Ol' Jube Early will be back tomorrow. You can bank on it."

After preparing camp, Silas ate supper with the rest of the troops. He waited a seeming eternity in the downpour for his meal. Sheridan had 48,000 soldiers under his command.

With a plateful of roasted beef, steaming corn, and all the apples he wanted, Silas entered his tent, dripping but elated. Virginia held a bounty of food at the Union's disposal.

Martin looked up from a magazine and smiled at him.

"I'm bunking with you, Corporal," he said. "Too many soldiers and not enough tents."

"Who's Applegate bunking with?"

"McCane. It was too crowded for the three of us. And you all by yourself!"

"Have you eaten?" Silas asked.

"Sure have. You are slow as molasses in January." Martin returned to his magazine. He was definitely back to normal.

"I can prove you wrong. Just watch me eat," Silas replied.

The rain stopped, but the ominous sky clued the men that the weather would most likely continue her disagreeability into tomorrow. Silas walked down to the creek to wash his plate and cup.

The waters of the Opequon Creek felt refreshingly cool in the humidity. The high pitched drone of cicadas sounded in the trees. Silas bent down and hastily swished water over his dishes. The air felt sticky and thick with heat. Silas dipped his hand in the cool water and splashed it on his face. He sensed the need to hurry back to the safety of his quarters, though hundreds of Union men swarmed nearby. He was over a thousand miles from the Red River, and still the Confederates lurked in the dense, rolling forests.

He saw a man in Union blue directly under the pole bearing the Stars and Stripes, mounted on a splendid black horse and surrounded by a half dozen aides, also on horseback. His black, secretive eyes reflected a certain coldness. His hair, also black, was neatly combed. A black moustache and small goatee fit low on his face, exposing high, chiseled cheekbones. He looked pleased and confident. He looked like a fighter.

Silas recognized the man at once.
He was Philip Sheridan.

.

Chapter Thirty-Three

August 31, 1864

Silas stood again as sentry. Three other pickets stood nearby. The morning had broken quietly, without rain, clouds, or Jubal Early. The Union soldiers remained inactive, nine miles from Harper's Ferry.

Why won't Sheridan fight? Silas wondered. So far they participated only in minor skirmishes. Silas knew they could whip Early's men. They were strong enough in number, rested, well fed, and determined. Yesterday Silas and his regiment had picked corn from the nearby fields for breakfast and apples from orchards that would supply the entire camp. Why was Sheridan taking pains to avoid a major conflict?

A battle was unavoidable. The Shenandoah Valley was too essential as one of the main breadbaskets of the Confederacy.

I guess he has his reasons, Silas thought.

After three hours of picket duty, his replacement came, a young private with a chubby face. Silas went into the cornfield to get his breakfast. Major Forsythe informed the men that if they wanted to eat, they would forage. On the way back to camp, Silas met up with a detail from the 28th Iowa. Martin was with them.

"Hey, we're going porking. Want to come?" Martin asked.

"There's a farm about three miles from here," McCane said.

"Sure," Silas said. Anything was better than sitting around. Besides, he hadn't eaten ham in ages. He reported back at camp, then followed the hunters into the forest. If General Sheridan persisted in inactivity, Silas could sleep when he returned. He wasn't tired, anyway.

They followed the creek, moving silently for protection from guerrilla soldiers who attacked Union stragglers almost daily. After months of marching twenty or thirty miles per day, they easily covered the three miles to the farm.

Silas looked at the farm and felt like he was home. Except for the woods surrounding it, the farm closely resembled his place in Clinton. War had taken its toll here, though. Fields were barren, the house and barn appeared worn, and there was no sign of life.

"Looks as though the Rebs already cleaned out this place," McCane whispered.

"The livestock might be hid somewhere," Silas said. "Come on. If there's a hog here, we'll find him."

Avoiding the clearing for the possibility of being seen from the house, the soldiers crept around to the back of the farm.

Walking single file, they searched the perimeter of the homestead but found nothing.

"Let's head back," Silas suggested.

They heard a shout, followed by a single gunshot. They tensed, scanning the woods that surrounded them.

"Where's Martin?" McCane asked.

Fearing the worst, Silas darted in the direction of the shot, the rest of the group at his heels.

He found Martin near a clearing by the creek, standing over a large hog. A broad grin stretched across Martin's face.

"I could use some help getting this porker back to camp," he said.

The six men dragged the heavy pig through the brush, stopping to rest every few minutes. Silas noticed that a trail of blood leaked behind them, possibly betraying their position to any Confederates in the area. Especially if the Rebs had heard Martin's shout.

"We need to hurry," Silas said.

They heard shots again.

"Hide!" Silas commanded. "Rebels!"

He crouched in the dense thicket with the rest of the men and waited. He heard more shots, realizing they came from the post he'd recently left. He stealthily parted the bush to get a better view.

Eight men in gray ran past, less than five feet away. Silas watched silently, holding his breath, until they disappeared.

"I think they're gone," he whispered after a few minutes.

"Wait a while," Martin whispered back. "I'm not moving until I know they're gone. I didn't shoot this hog for nothing."

Silas nodded. Sheridan might send the cavalry after the guerrillas, and he didn't want to get in the way. The cavalry was undoubtedly Sheridan's greatest strength. They waited.

The only sound was flies around the animal corpse.

"Let's go. We're close enough to make a run for it," McCane said.

Silas walked ahead, his rifle poised, his eyes scanning the sylvan landscape for flashes of gray.

They stepped over the dead body of the guard who had replaced Silas on picket.

A new sentry was already posted. Ahead, Silas saw men coming to take the body.

"An hour sooner and it would've been you, Cross," Martin said solemnly. "Good thing the Rebs slept in this morning."

Silas didn't reply. He didn't want to think about it.

Chapter Thirty-Four

September 10, 1864

"Hey, Silas, we're taking an informal poll," Martin told him.

Silas was busy preparing for drill. Autumn approached, bringing fiery displays of changing leaves and cool weather from the north.

"What poll?" Silas asked.

"Are you for Abe, McClellan, or Fremont?"

"I can't vote," Silas said. "I'm only twenty."

"Well, that don't matter," Martin insisted. "This is informal. Come on, who you for?"

"Lincoln."

"Good choice. Me, too."

"Martin," Silas gave him a disagreeable look, "you're not trying to persuade anyone to lean your way, are you?"

"No. I wouldn't do a thing like that. Besides," he grinned again. "I don't have to. Most of the men are for Abe. In fact, it looks to me as though Lincoln is going to win by a landslide."

"How many votes for Abe?" Silas asked, suddenly interested.

Martin pulled out a letter he received from home.

He had written the numbers on the back with a lead pencil.

"Lincoln—338. McClellan—7. Fremont—21. Company E wouldn't vote. Said it was nonsense."

Silas knew many of the men in Company E. "They are mostly for Lincoln," he said.

The bugle sounded. Silas and Martin grabbed their Springfields and headed to the center of camp for their daily drill practice, now required by Sheridan.

General Sheridan stood beside Generals Emory, Ord, and Grover as the mass of soldiers lined up in the clearing.

"Men, I have just received a dispatch from General Grant," Sheridan said in a confidant, booming voice. The men listened respectfully to their small but capable commander. "Sherman has captured Atlanta."

A rousing cheer erupted from the troops.

It was glorious news.

Maybe, Silas thought, this blasted war will end after all.

CHAPTER THIRTY-FIVE

September 18 , 1864

"General Grant is in camp!" Martin exclaimed after his relief from sentry duty late in the morning. Everyone in camp knew Grant and Sheridan had met day before yesterday at Sheridan's headquarters. Now, to everyone's elation, Grant was in their midst.

Silas hoped to get a look at the commander. Though he served under Grant in Vicksburg, he had never seen the general. Grant was as famous as Lincoln. Silas put down his pencil and closed his diary, which he had been keeping for many months.

"He's going to be present at dress parade," Martin went on. "I heard Captain Carr tell Lieutenant Dran."

Silas felt a strange blend of excitement and foreboding. With Grant in camp, something was bound to happen. "Unconditional Surrender" Grant meant to end the war as quickly as possible, and Lincoln was no doubt dogging him to do so, with the election so close. Sheridan and Grant were most certainly planning a battle strategy right now, if they hadn't already done it.

Thousands of Union soldiers, dressed in clean uniforms and carrying polished weapons, stood in their separate regiments, the high ranking officers in front. As they paraded to the fifer's and drummer's march, Silas caught a glimpse of the man standing next to Philip Sheridan.

He stood, round shouldered, a scruffy, rather short man of undefined, regular features. He puffed nonchalantly on a cigar. Much of his face was hidden by a full, brown beard. His clear blue eyes, though, exposed his character to anyone who took the time to look at them. They showed grit and determination.

"Did you get a look at him?" Silas asked Martin as they prepared supper. Silas's new mess group consisted of Applegate, McCane, Martin, and himself.

"He's a hard old cuss," Martin said.

"Lee is sunk," McCane replied. "Grant and Sheridan together will follow him like vicious dogs, devouring his army a few at a time until none are left to fight back."

"You're right," Silas agreed. "It's only a matter of time." And I hope we can hang on and survive until that time, he thought.

* *

The Army of the James moved at two a.m. They marched silently in the darkness toward Winchester.

Silas knew Sheridan wasn't waiting any longer. Today they would give battle to Jubal Early. As they passed through Berryville, a small town near the Shenandoah River, he watched the sunrise. He wondered, without fear or remorse, if he would ever see another.

120

CHAPTER THIRTY-SIX

September 19, 1864

At ten a.m. they neared Winchester, crossing the Opequon Creek downstream from where they camped several days ago.

Sheridan's cavalry, a tough, well-trained group of riders, charged ahead. They disappeared into the dense woods, riding proudly with straight backs and high chins. Silas watched them until they were out of sight. Sheridan loved his cavalry like his own sons. The infantry did not share the sentiment, Silas included.

Silas marched along the stone pike with the rest of the infantry. In the distance he heard gunfire and the boom of artillery. Ahead, like the recurrence of the bad dream of Sabine Crossroads, wagons blocked the way, a hindrance to the thousands of soldiers behind.

Sheridan rode up to General Emory and swore mightily, words Silas never dreamed of saying.

"Get those wagons out of the way!! Immediately!!" Sheridan roared.

"Where shall I put them, sir?" Emory asked.

"In the ditch!" Sheridan yelled. "Early will have all the divisions from Virginia coming to his rescue by the time we get there! It will destroy the element of surprise!

My cavalry are sitting ducks!"

Quickly the carts were strewn aside.

Silas found himself, along with the rest of his regiment, on the left flank in an attempt to halt a Confederate escape.

"Double quick, men! March!" came the order and the Federals began to run.

Shells exploded and bullets whistled. The all-too-familiar smoke stung Silas's eyes and made him gasp for breath. Surrounded by hundreds of soldiers like himself, Silas ran boldly on, his bayonet protruding from his Springfield like a deadly banner.

In the forest they grouped in columns, taking refuge behind trees and shrubs.

"Hold this spot, men!" General Emory yelled as Rebels burst from the foliage.

They collided with the soldiers—mostly grays with a few butternut uniforms in the midst—and began fighting furiously. Men fell everywhere as the pandemonium of bullets and shells burst from every direction.

A tall blond Rebel, obviously an officer in his gray finery, galloped up on horseback.

"Penetrate the breach!" he shouted. A bullet caught him in the chest with such force that it knocked the handsome Confederate off his steed.

Silas looked down the Union line. A gaping hole from the last volley of cannon had opened up the ranks.

"Close the gap!" Emory ordered, his voice ringing with authority. The soldiers immediately obeyed as best they could under the constant fire raining upon them.

Jubal Early fought stubbornly as the sun glared down upon the fight. The battlefield filled with bodies of the dead. Silas fought on, the fatigue overtaking the strange exhilaration that rushed through his veins.

Finally, the Rebels withdrew as quickly as they had come. The Battle of Winchester, a Union victory, was over.

Chapter Thirty-Seven

October 7, 1864

Silas sat beside the campfire eating roasted mutton. After the battle at Winchester, the soldiers spent most of their time foraging and burning. The constant rain couldn't slow the determined Sheridan and his men, who marched from town to town on the stone pike.

In the distance Silas could see the fire from ill-fated barns and mills. Smoke, though cloaked in the night, permeated the camp with acrid smells.

"The Sixth Corps found a bunch of hay in the barns," Applegate said to the others as he ate. "We'll have hay to sleep on tonight."

"Sounds good to me," Silas said glad to have the Sixth Corps on loan from Meade's army. "I'm tired of wet ground and leaky tents."

"Me, too," Martin agreed. "I think our tent is the leakiest one around."

Silas smiled. Martin was right. Their tent dripped steadily in a half dozen places the last few days. At least straw would keep them warm in the increasingly cool nights.

After dinner a group of men, including Silas's Company C, appeared before Colonel Slack.

"You have your orders," he said. "You know what to do."

"Yes, sir," a recently promoted Captain Elza saluted. He was a handsome man with kind brown eyes and graying hair.

The body of soldiers crept down to the Shenandoah River in the darkness. The clouds above them parted, allowing a glimpse of faraway stellar seas.

Working quickly, Silas took explosives from the crate and passed them on. Martin broke the keg of gunpowder and placed the keg under the bridge. Captain Elza gave the order and Silas lit the fuse.

Sparks sprang to life in the blackness. After a momentary silence the gunpowder detonated, and in a brilliant flash of light, the bridge collapsed.

Silas thought the explosion the grandest he'd ever seen.

Chapter Thirty-Eight

October 19, 1864

Silas awoke with the rest of his regiment at four a.m. and stood at arms. Since they had reached Cedar Creek yesterday, all was quiet. But Silas, along with the entire army, knew the Rebels waited nearby. Though other Union men lay sleeping, exhausted from yesterday's march, the 28th Iowa prepared for battle.

The Rebels attacked at dawn, obviously hoping to catch the Union by surprise. For many, the ruse worked. Soldiers leaped from tents, some half-dressed. The fighting began in great ferocity.

The boom of artillery rumbled through the foggy Virginia countryside. Silas's brogans were wet with dew. He slipped twice on the grass as he ran to keep up with the rest of the regiment. The fog and smoke enveloped him, giving him the sense of being in an eerie dream.

He heard the simultaneous blast of gunfire, followed by cries of anguish. He was certain he recognized one of the screams.

"Martin!" he yelled.

No answer.

He ran on in the mist, not daring to fire until he could see his target. He listened to moans beneath him and knew he was near his own men.

Suddenly men in blue burst from the fog. The frightening Rebel yell resounded through the air.

Applegate appeared in the hordes of fleeing soldiers.

"Retreat, Cross!" he screamed. "They've broken through the lines! They're flanking us!"

Silas fell back with his regiment. I'll retreat, he thought, but I'll get a shot off before I do.

Silas ran through the confusion, stopping momentarily to peer through the dense haze. He spotted a butternut and took quick aim.

He heard the *whizz* of a bullet and a sickening thud. The impact knocked him to the ground. His right arm burned as though it were consumed with flames. He looked down and saw blood.

I'm hit, he thought desperately.

Men stampeded by him, nearly trampling him as he struggled to keep from giving in to the shock.

I have to get back, he thought.

Silas blinked, forcing himself out of the compelling inertia. He was abruptly aware of someone standing over him.

"Get up, Yank," the voice said.

Silas peered through the grayness and focused on three men. Two wore homespun butternut, the other Confederate gray. All three pointed muskets at his chest.

Silas slowly rose to his feet. Blood saturated his sleeve and spilled over onto his torso.

"Get his rifle," the man in gray commanded. "Looks like a new one. We can use it."

The two butternuts grabbed Silas and pulled him toward their lines. The one on his right picked up his Springfield.

Silas trudged through the meadow, his heart sick with uncertainty. He didn't want to live out the rest of the war in prison. Horror stories abounded with tales of Andersonville in Georgia and Libby Prison in Richmond. He grimly realized that he might not survive there. The healthy had a hard enough time doing it. The wounded almost never made it.

Suddenly cheers broke through the desolation. Silas heard the chant.

"Sheridan, Sheridan."

Sheridan had arrived from his quarters in Martinsburg. The Federal troops were rallying.

Silas tried to walk more slowly. The Rebels pulled him mercilessly along. He winced in pain but refused to cry out.

"Hurry!" the man in gray said to the others. "Sheridan is here. The Yankees are coming back!"

Silas slumped to the ground.

"I can't," he gasped, clutching his torso and right arm with his left.

"Leave him!" the graycoat ordered. "He's badly wounded. He'll die anyway."

The butternuts dropped him and vanished into the woods.

Silas lay in the tall grass, exultant.

His performance had worked.

CHAPTER THIRTY-NINE

December 11, 1864

Silas stood in the cold twilight before Captain Elza's tent. He caught a glimpse of the captain between the flaps. Elza was sitting at his desk, writing a letter by candlelight.

"Sir?" he asked quietly.

Captain Elza looked up from his writing. He smiled.

"Come in, Corporal."

Silas entered the tent and removed his hat. He stood before the captain.

"Please, sit down," Captain Elza offered, gesturing to the chair beside his desk.

Silas sat down.

"How's the arm?"

"It's much better, thank you, sir," Silas said, moving his healed arm at the elbow. It still felt stiff, but only a little.

"Well, good. What can I do for you?"

Silas took a small book from his side pocket. Since Cedar Creek he had talked a few times with Captain Elza about the war, and he had mentioned his diary. Captain Elza had invited him to read it to him whenever he had the chance.

"Ah, your diary," the captain replied. "Are you going to read some more to me?"

"Well, no sir," Silas said. "I mean, I will if you'd like, but I . . ." He struggled to find the words. He felt no foreboding, but he wanted to be sure the diary found its way home should he not get there himself. His life existed — would always exist — in these pages, and he wanted his family to have it. So much had changed since Cedar Creek. Colonel Slack was gone, and Captain Carr took his place over the regiment. Sergeant Jones was gone, sent home maimed for life, and Sergeant Brannan replaced him. Martin had survived the battle, but lost his right foot. He behaved morosely for weeks, but finally began acting like himself again after Lincoln won the November election by a landslide. Silas visited him at the hospital until he was well enough to go home. Home. The word sounded almost foreign to Silas. He wondered if he would ever see Clinton, Iowa, again.

"Silas. What is it?" Captain Elza asked gently.

"I was just wondering, sir," Silas said, "if something should happen to me, will you see to it that my folks back home get this?" He held up the small diary, its binding worn, its pages fat from use.

Captain Elza looked at him with fatherly concern.

"Son," he said, "I will do that. But don't worry. You'll be reading pages of that book to your folks yourself. I'm sure of it."

Silas nodded. He wished he felt as sure.

Captain Elza stared at the letter on his desk, apparently lost in thought.

"Who would have guessed we'd be spending another Christmas in the trenches," he said, his voice almost a whisper. "I haven't seen my family in so long."

Silas managed a smile. Inside he felt lonely. Sad. Doomed to march and fight forever.

"Mosby's out there trying to get us into trouble," Elza went on. "He attacked the cavalry last night. They just don't give up, those Rebs."

Silas shook his head. The redoubtable Rebel guerilla Mosby. The Rebs were devoted to their cause, no doubt about that. He stroked the cover of the diary.

"Well, thank you, Captain."

"Good night, Silas. I'm glad you have kept a record. I wish I had." He sighed. "I always thought I was too busy." He gave a short laugh and Silas smiled out of respect. "We've lived a page of history. Several pages, in fact."

Silas saluted. "Good night, sir."

He left the tent and stepped out into the night. The snow halfway covered his leg. He looked up and saw the stars. No clouds. It would be cold tonight.

He headed for his tent, passing the gentle glow of candles inside the almost invisible tents hidden by snow. He glanced up into the endless dark.

He was living a page of history.

Well, he thought, I'll gladly exchange it with anyone who wants it.

CHAPTER FORTY

December 31, 1864

Silas sat in his tent somewhere in Russell County, Virginia. He rested in his blanket on the straw-covered floor, struggling to remain warm since coming off picket at two p.m. He spent the afternoon writing to his mother and father and then a long letter to Keckley. Dinner again had been scant, but the hot coffee warmed him.

He looked outside. Snow drifted across the blanket of white that enveloped the camp. There were at least four inches out there now. That was better than last week. Before Christmas he measured a full foot of snow on the ground.

He absentmindedly rubbed his frostbitten toe. He had accidentally uncovered it last night in his sleep, but at least his arm had healed.

Martin had not fared as well. Poor Martin. But he had survived at least. Silas wondered if he would see Martin, or Keck, again. If he made it home, he would find them. Applegate suffered a leg wound at Cedar Creek and was promoted to Corporal. McCane had made it through unscathed. Silas was relieved that all of them were alive.

Silas flipped through the pages of his small diary, now full of the days of 1864.

The sun began to set early. In the cloudy haze Silas couldn't see the sun, but as darkness approached he felt the effects of the day's—and the year's—demise. Night waited beyond the horizon to overtake them just as Rebels had in the woods and bayous. As the last night of 1864 crept over the camp, Silas lay back in his blanket and remembered.

Somewhere in camp Silas heard the fiddler. He played expertly, the strings singing softly, like an ethereal being. Silas recognized the tune and felt his throat tighten.

Should auld acquaintance be forgot
And never brought to mind,
Should auld acquaintance be forgot
In the days of auld lang syne . . .

Silas listened. He was certain the troops knew "Auld Lang Syne" as well as he did, yet no one sang. Tonight marked Silas's third New Year's Eve in the army, but this time, he couldn't bring himself to sing. The words fell too closely to his heart.

For auld lang syne, my dear
For auld lang syne,
We'll take a cup of kindness yet
For auld lang syne!

In his mind, he saw his family. He saw Henry, Keckley, Joe, and Conner. He remembered the last time he talked to Anthony in the surgeon's tent, and Martin peering through Silas's tent, sunburned and grinning, asking him to go swimming with the alligators. He felt the breeze off Lake Pontchartrain and the steamy heat of New

Orleans in the summer. He recalled the Alexandria belle and her angry eyes. He remembered the pain in his arm as the Rebels at Cedar Creek nearly carried him off to languish in some rotted hole the Confederates called prison. He could see Mount Vernon on the Potomac and hear the squirrels chatter. It was part of his life that was gone forever, and dear friends along with it.

As the last shred of gray light surrendered to the dark, Silas thought about the color gray. It reflected the shades of all right and wrong. Every aspect of government and patriotism flowed into the color.

He believed in the Union. He felt confident that he fought for the right thing.

But, somewhere in the Shenandoah Valley, probably singing Auld Lang Syne as well, were people who felt differently. They fought for their homes and a way of life that would soon go where past years were laid to rest.

How fitting that gray colored the uniform of the Confederacy.

Tonight the sun sets on 1864, he thought, and tomorrow the sun rises on 1865.

What would 1865 bring? Silas had no idea.

He would take it one day at a time.

Epilogue

Silas Newton Cross survived the War Between the States. He went home to Clinton, Iowa, and enjoyed a long-awaited reunion with his family. He married in 1867. He and his wife, Telia, settled in Lawton, Oklahoma, where Silas owned a restaurant and inn. They had six children.

Silas died on September 18, 1918, of heart disease, at the age of seventy-four.

He was one of the lucky ones. Over 620,000 men, North and South, never came home.